❖

GARDENS OF THE
HUDSON RIVER VALLEY

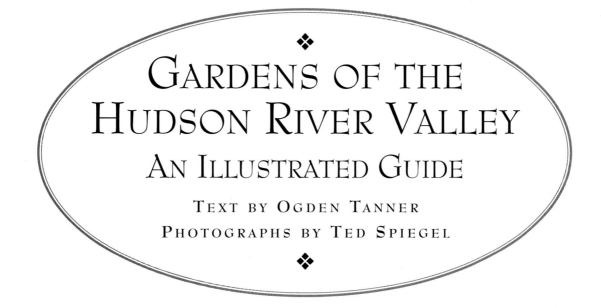

Gardens of the Hudson River Valley
An Illustrated Guide

Text by Ogden Tanner
Photographs by Ted Spiegel

Harry N. Abrams, Inc., Publishers,
in association with
Friends of the Hudson Valley

This book is dedicated to Laurance S. Rockefeller for his interest and support.

EDITOR: RUTH A. PELTASON
DESIGNERS: RAYMOND P. HOOPER, DIRK LUYKX, JENNIFER DAVENPORT
MAP: CHRISTINE V. EDWARDS

Front cover: A view of the perennial garden at the Mary Flagler Cary Arboretum in Millbrook.
Back cover: "The Meadow" at Innisfree in Millbrook.
Page 2: The formal rose garden, seen off the side entrance to the Boscobel mansion, located in Garrison.

Library of Congress Cataloging-in-Publication Data
Tanner, Ogden.
Gardens of the Hudson River Valley : an illustrated guide / text
by Ogden Tanner ; photographs by Ted Spiegel.
p.   cm.
ISBN 0–8109–2643–1 (pbk.)
1. Gardens—Hudson River Valley (N.Y. and N.J.)—Guidebooks.
2. Hudson River Valley (N.Y. and N.J.)—Guidebooks.   I. Spiegel,
Ted.   II. Title.
SB466.U65N7437   1996
712'.5'097473—dc20   95–24698

Copyright © Friends of the Hudson Valley

Published in 1996 by Harry N. Abrams, Incorporated, New York
A Times Mirror Company
No part of the contents of this book may be reproduced without the written permission
of the publisher

Printed and bound in Singapore

About the Authors

Ogden Tanner,
a prize-winning garden writer and a former editor of Time-Life Books,
has written *The New York Botanical Garden,* a centennial portrait, and
Gardening America, a survey of regional landscaping styles.

Ted Spiegel,
a well-known photographer, is a contributor to *National Geographic*.
Three of his books explore the beauty of the Hudson Valley:
An American Treasure, Saratoga, and *West Point*. Friends of the Hudson
Valley publishes his Hudson River Valley calendar annually.

CONTENTS

INTRODUCTION

❖

A LIVING TREASURE

There is no part of the Union where the taste in Landscape Gardening is so far advanced. —Andrew Jackson Downing, 1841

Compared to the Mississippi or the Nile, the Hudson is not very long. But it may be the most *interesting* river in the world. Indeed, in its 150-mile stretch from New York City to Albany, the Hudson, like the grand dowager she is, wears a necklace of scenic and horticultural gems that would be hard to match anywhere else. The valley is not only the cradle of America's most famous school of painting, the Hudson River School; it also gave birth to nationwide movements for conservation and public parks and to the emergence of landscape architecture as an art form that would change the face of the American countryside.

Over the years the river's mountainous beauty has inspired an extraordinary variety of man-made landscapes, each a distinctive expression of its time and place. In this book we have chosen some of the most notable ones, ranging from the utilitarian gardens of early settlers to great sculpture parks commissioned by patrons of modern art. In visiting them, one experiences more than pretty flowers and stunning river views. One samples the sweep of history.

Beginning in the 1600s and 1700s, Dutch patroons and their English successors vied to establish private empires along the river's banks; their way of life is echoed in country seats like Philipsburg Manor in North Tarrytown, Van Cortlandt Manor in Croton, Clermont in Germantown, and Montgomery Place in Annandale.

With the age of Romanticism in the 1800s, the valley fairly bloomed.

Washington Irving created Sunnyside, his picturesque "snuggery" in Tarrytown. Artist Frederic Church built Olana, a fanciful hilltop retreat near the town of Hudson that combined his passion for painting, landscaping, and architecture into a single work of art. Near New Paltz, the Smiley brothers erected Mohonk Mountain House, a rambling lakeside resort beloved by visitors for its stunning Victorian gardens, rustic gazebos, and scenic walking trails.

Meanwhile, new generations of millionaires had launched their own gilded era of Hudson Valley estates, among them Lyndhurst in Tarrytown, Kykuit in Pocantico Hills, Wethersfield in Amenia, and William Vanderbilt's opulent mansion in Hyde Park, each notable for gardens on a lavish scale. Many of the old estates have been adapted to new cultural ends. Caramoor in Katonah is famous for its music festivals; Wave Hill in Riverdale, Skylands in Ringwood, and the former Cary estate in Millbrook have become renowned for their educational gardens and arboretums. The Storm King Art Center, a former millionaire's retreat in Mountainville, has been developed as a spacious setting for major twentieth-century sculpture.

Still other landscapes are the products of individual visions. The Cloisters in upper Manhattan is an authentic assemblage of the medieval art and courtyard gardens that John D. Rockefeller, Jr., admired. At Manitoga in Garrison, industrial designer Russel Wright created a "forest garden" that would allow people to experience nature in an intensely personal way. Innisfree in Millbrook reflects Walter and Marion Beck's own view of nature as a series of oriental pictures within the larger frame of a magnificent, hill-girt lake. Opus 40 in Saugerties is an immense land

Thomas Cole.
The Pic-nic. *1846.*
Oil on canvas, 44⅞ × 71⅞".
The Brooklyn Museum,
A. Augustus Healy Fund
B. 67.205.2

form of quarry stones, laid by the hands of a single artist, Harvey Fite. Mountain Top Arboretum in Tannersville realizes a dream of Peter and Bonnie Ahrens to grow and study a wide variety of plants. The PepsiCo headquarters in Purchase, the vision of CEO Donald Kendall, is a modern corporate Versailles that combines the finest in architecture, sculpture, and horticultural design.

And so the celebration, and democratization, of the Hudson Valley has taken many forms. Particularly revealing is Albany, where three landscapes evoke quite different themes in the region's history. Washington Park epitomizes the dreams of nineteenth-century romantics and the so-called civilizing influence of nature that they hoped public parks would bring. The Nelson A. Rockefeller Empire State Plaza is a vast, futuristic esplanade of fountains and skyscrapers, a sort of twentieth century "people's park." Often overlooked in the Plaza's shadow is a tiny garden in nearby Academy Park. Planted by ordinary citizens who wanted to help beautify their city, it is the newest garden, and it is centered on the valley's oldest, loveliest heritage: the native wild flowers of New York State.

An engraved poster of 1893 shows ladies and gentlemen enjoying a summers' day at Mohonk Mountain House, whose elaborate porches and turrets rise at right.

In their richness and variety, these gardens constitute a national treasure, one that more and more Americans enjoy each year. Earlier in this century the region continued its land-use pioneering by inventing the idea of parkways, whose prototypes eventually led to scenic, limited-access highways all over the United States.

Today a broader, even more ambitious idea is afoot: the concept of a

INTRODUCTION

greenway to link the Hudson's many natural and historic jewels into large, contiguous preserves of scenic open space graced by leisurely pedestrian paths.

It could be the Hudson Valley's greatest accomplishment to date—a landscape of landscapes, a necklace of gems, on a truly regional scale.

❖ NOTE TO THE READER: For the traveler's convenience, the gardens and landscapes in this book are organized into four sections, proceeding from New York City north to Albany. Within each section, sites are also grouped from south to north so that several can be visited in the course of a trip. Directions for train travel are given from New York's Grand Central Station unless otherwise stated; for schedule and fare information please call Metro-North (212) 532-4900.

Frederic Church. Landscape, Hudson Valley. 1870. Oil and graphite on cardboard, 11⅛ × 15¼". Courtesy of the Cooper-Hewitt, National Design Museum, Smithsonian Institution, New York. Gift of Louis P. Church

INTRODUCTION

❖

THE CONSERVATORY GARDEN, CENTRAL PARK

Carved out of Central Park's bosky landscape, the Central Garden (left) has allées of Siberian crab apples leading to a fountain, which is dominated by an arc-shaped pergola of wisteria vines. The North Garden (right), laid out in classical French style, features another fountain bordered by beds of tulips in spring and chrysanthemums in fall.

Tucked away in the northeastern corner of Manhattan's Central Park is one of the city's least known treasures: an enclave of gardens whose classic design contrasts sharply with the rest of the park's rambling, naturalistic contours. Here, only a few steps below the bustle of Fifth Avenue traffic, visitors can stroll down peaceful allées of flowering crab apples, admire brilliant seasonal displays of tulips and chrysanthemums, pause in a "secret garden" of perennials where children listen to stories by a water lily pool.

The Conservatory Garden takes its name from a complex of Victorian greenhouses that once stood on the spot, attracting swarms of visitors from their opening in 1899. During the Depression in 1934, the glass houses were torn down because of their high maintenance costs. With the help of federal WPA funds, they were replaced by a triptych of formal gardens, designed by the Parks Department with Gilmore D. Clarke as consulting landscape architect and planting plans by M. Betty Sprout.

By the late 1970s, due to the city's recurring financial difficulties, the gardens, like much of Central Park, had fallen into disrepair. Enter the New York Committee of the Garden Club of America, whose volunteers began to tend the plants and raise money to repair the broken fountains. In 1982 a major restoration started with a grant from Rockefeller Center to the Central Park Conservancy, which replanted the South Garden with 3,500 perennials in beds redesigned by Lynden B. Miller,

THE CONSERVATORY GARDEN,
CENTRAL PARK

appointed as the Conservatory Garden's director. Permanent maintenance was ensured by the generosity of the Weiler-Arnow family, which provided $1.5 million in endowment funds.

Visitors to the refurbished garden enter from Fifth Avenue at 105th Street through the ornate, wrought-iron Vanderbilt Gate, made for the Vanderbilt mansion down the avenue at 58th Street and given to the city after the mansion was torn down. Immediately below the steps lies the Central Garden, a half-acre rectangle of lawn flanked by allées of Siberian crab apples—rare Hyslop varieties whose picturesquely twisted branches burst into clouds of pink and white blooms in early May, accompanied by narcissuses poking up through beds of ivy.

Furnished with decorative park benches from the 1939 New York World's Fair, the allées lead to a jetting central fountain, a favorite spot for newlyweds to have their pictures taken. Behind the fountain, semicircular hedges flanked by steps rise to an upper terrace and pergola covered by half-century-old wisteria vines, whose long clusters of blue, pea-flowered blooms appear in late May.

The adjoining North Garden is laid out in classical French style, with circular beds around another fountain, *The Three Dancing Maidens* by sculptor Walter Schott, given by the Untermeyer family. This garden is renowned for its seasonal displays—20,000 tulips in spring and 5,000 chrysanthemums in fall—and for its arbors covered in 'Silver Moon', an old climbing rose that puts forth luminous white blossoms in June. Surrounding the beds are many handsome flowering shrubs, among them salmon-colored Japanese quince, white spirea, and two ever-blooming roses, 'The Fairy', with pink blossoms, and 'Seafoam', whose flowers are white.

The South Garden was designed to provide quite a different experience, and, for dedicated gardeners, a textbook of perennials suitable to the region. This garden also centers on a fountain, adorned by Bessie Potter Vonnoh's charming statues of two children from *The Secret Garden*, the classic by Frances Hodgson Burnett. The fountain pool is planted with tropical water lilies that bloom through the summer; behind benches that serve for reading and storytelling are ranks of 'Betty Prior' roses, an old-fashioned, long-blooming variety whose pink flowers stand

14

The South Garden centers on a water-lily pool and Bessie Potter Vonnoh's sculpture of two children from the classic The Secret Garden.

out against dark green barberry hedges. Surrounding these in concentric, horseshoe-shaped beds is a striking collection of perennials—some 175 kinds chosen to provide continuous color, from the small yellowish sprays of lady's mantle in early spring to the rust-colored flower heads of Sedum 'Autumn Joy'. Enclosing the display are lilac trees whose purple and white flowers perfume the air in May.

On a hillside above, visitors can enjoy the Conservatory Garden's newest addition: the Woodland Slope, where plantings were begun in 1984 following Penelope Maynard's designs. Here grow hundreds of ferns and wild flowers, including mayapples, wild geraniums, Virginia bluebells, and forget-me-nots.

❖ THE CONSERVATORY GARDEN, Central Park, Fifth Avenue and 105th Street. For information, contact the Central Park Conservancy, 830 Fifth Avenue, New York, NY 10121. Tel. (212) 860-1382. **Facilities**: Sitting benches, rest rooms. Accessible to the handicapped through northwest gate; enter at 106th Street. **Open**: Daily, 8 a.m. to dusk. Admission free. **Directions**: No public parking lot in the park, and parking is limited on nearby streets, so public transportation is recommended.

THE CONSERVATORY GARDEN, CENTRAL PARK

❖

THE CLOISTERS,
FORT TRYON PARK

The northern tip of Manhattan might seem an improbable site for a medieval monastery, but John D. Rockefeller, Jr., knew what he liked. He also had the money to make his dreams come true.

More than a half century ago, Rockefeller, an avid promoter of public parks, had purchased the heights that were once used for Revolutionary War fortifications and presented them to the city as Fort Tryon Park. He had also bought an impressive collection of European art and architectural fragments and assembled them in the Cloisters, a unique museum of medieval life that opened to the public in 1938. A man of foresight, John D., Jr., even helped acquire a scenic section of the Palisades across the Hudson, making sure that the magnificent view from the hilltop would never be spoiled.

Among the Cloisters' priceless displays are four courtyard gardens that reflect the museum's name. At the center of the main level is the Cuxa Cloister, whose covered arcades, salvaged from a twelfth-century Benedictine monastery in the Pyrenees, surround a garth or enclosed yard. In such yards medieval monks took time off from their duties to enjoy a breath of fresh air, to meditate, to copy manuscripts or wash their clothes. The plan is typical: crossed paths and a central fountain dividing the area into four grassy beds, each with a flowering tree—pear, hawthorn, crab apple, cornelian cherry—bordered by plantings that include Madonna lilies, lavender, and asters.

In winter the Cuxa's open arcades are enclosed in glass and filled with pots of rosemary, jasmine, citrus, acanthus, aloe, and bay. Here bulbs like narcissus, lily of the valley, and grape hyacinth are also forced into bloom, then transferred to the nearby Saint-Guilhem Cloister, an indoor garden where the plants are grouped around a fountain to provide dis-

Above: An aerial view of the Cloisters, with the Hudson River and the George Washington Bridge in the background. Left: The Bonnefont Cloister contains some 250 species of plants used in the Middle Ages for vegetables, salads, seasonings, dyes, and household herbs, as well as fruiting quince trees located in central beds.

THE CLOISTERS, FORT TRYON PARK

plays from Christmas through Easter.

On a lower level, the Bonnefont Cloister illustrates the many uses of plants in the Middle Ages. Arranged around an old well, in symmetrical beds edged with brick and wattles, are some 250 species, grouped by use—vegetable and salad plants, kitchen seasonings, medicinal herbs, dye plants, and aromatic, cosmetic, and household herbs, along with ornamental plants and old roses like *Rosa alba* and apothecary's rose. In four central beds are fruiting quince trees, underplanted with cowslip, sweet cicely, sweet woodruff, and lily of the valley. Below one wall of the garden a small orchard of crab apples bursts with pink and white blossoms in spring.

Adjoining the Bonnefont Cloister is the smaller Trie Cloister, a floral whimsy that duplicates in living form most of the plants depicted in the museum's famous Unicorn Tapestries. Among them are lilies, carnations, bluebells, primroses, violets, and wild strawberries. At the center is a fountain surmounted by a tall limestone cross carved with figures of Christ, the Virgin and Child, and various saints. Like the other gardens of the Cloisters, this one is endowed in perpetuity by Enid A. Haupt, something of a floral saint herself.

❖ THE CLOISTERS, Fort Tryon Park, New York, NY 10040. Tel. (212) 923-3700. A branch of The Metropolitan Museum of Art. **Facilities:** Sitting areas, gift shop, rest rooms. Limited access to the handicapped; call ahead. **Open:** Tuesday through Sunday, 9:30 a.m. to 5:15 p.m., March through October; 9:30 a.m. to 4:45 p.m., November through February. Closed Mondays and New Year's Day, Thanksgiving, and Christmas. Admission free to Metropolitan Museum of Art members; suggested donation for others. **Directions:** By car from Manhattan or New Jersey, take the Henry Hudson Parkway to the first exit north of the George Washington Bridge; from the north, take Henry Hudson Parkway south, exit left lane under George Washington Bridge, left again and north on Henry Hudson Parkway to first exit. By subway, take the IND Eighth Avenue A train to 190th Street, then No. 4 bus to Fort Tryon Park-The Cloisters. By bus, take the Madison Avenue No. 4 to Fort Tryon Park.

*The focal point of the Trie
Cloister is a fountain and a
limestone cross with figures of
Christ, the Virgin and Child,
and various saints.*

THE CLOISTERS, FORT TRYON PARK

❖

THE NEW YORK BOTANICAL GARDEN, BRONX

The New York Botanical Garden—250 acres of gardens, plant collections, fields, and woodlands in the heart of the Bronx—is not only a fine place for a day's outing. It is also a living nature museum where even sophisticated gardeners can learn a great deal about the world of plants.

Of more than a score of gardens at the NYBG, each organized on a different theme, the most venerable is not a garden in the usual sense. It is a magnificent 40-acre forest, the only major patch remaining from a vast woodland that once covered most of metropolitan New York. Here trails wander along the gorge of the Bronx River among beeches, red oaks, and tulip trees where a surprising variety of wildlife abounds.

Among the most popular gardens is the Thomas H. Everett Rock Garden, designed and built by the NYBG's director of horticulture beginning in 1932. Today it boasts close to a thousand species and varieties in several collections, each illustrating the use of different plants in different habitats.

Adjacent to the Rock Garden is the Native Plant Garden, displaying species indigenous to the Northeastern U.S. A moist, sunny central meadow shows off Joe-Pye weed, goldenrod, butterflyweed, ironweed, and Turk's-cap lily. On one fringe are plants common to the pine barrens of New Jersey and Long Island, including bearberry, pitch pine and sand myrtle. Wooded areas above the meadow are devoted to early-blooming wild flowers—bloodroot, trillium, lady's-slipper orchids—and to the F. Gordon Foster Hardy Fern Collection, some 200 species and varieties that include native types and others from similar climates around the world.

The Native Plant Garden also highlights a grouping of wild perennials that make fine garden plants: black-eyed Susan, New England aster, cardinal flower, bee balm, purple coneflower. A small bog features native

water lilies, aquatic irises, and marsh marigolds. A rocky limestone area displays American twinleaf, shooting star, crested iris, and columbine.

From the Rock and Native Plant Gardens, a path leads north to Rhododendron Valley, which boasts many Dexter hybrids, including the fragrant pink 'Scintillation', one of the most widely popular rhododendrons today. The valley also features the Murray Liasson Narcissus Collection, some 20,000 bulbs of more than 100 types that not only provide striking spring displays but serve as a useful reference to the many varieties suitable for growing in the region.

To the south is Azalea Way, which reaches its peak of color in May with torch azaleas, yellow azaleas, Korean azaleas, pink-shell azaleas, orange flame azaleas, and royal azaleas. Other paths lead to a collection of improved varieties of crab apples that bloom in shades of white, pink, and red. To the west is Daffodil Hill, where in April tens of thousands of plants form bright blankets on the slopes.

Beyond a bridge over the Bronx River are more gardens, among them the Robert H. Montgomery Conifer Collection and the large Peggy Rockefeller Rose Garden, whose formal beds, radiating out from a central gazebo, contain 2,700 plants of some 230 species and cultivars, including a hundred varieties of old garden and shrub roses like Bourbon, Damask, Gallica, Centifolia, Rugosa, Moss, and Hybrid Musk.

To the north of the rose garden is the Havemeyer Lilac Collection, where 90 species and cultivars of lilacs bloom in late spring, their purple, lavender, pink, and white flowers perfuming the air. Directly opposite is Cherry Valley, where trees include rosebud cherries and Japanese flowering types. At the crest of the hill is the Arlow B. Stout Daylily Garden, a collection of 120 day lily species and cultivars that commemorate Stout's outstanding achievements with the genus *Hemerocallis* while working as a botanist at the NYBG. Included are many of his own cultivars, among them 'Theron', the first dark red day lily, which took Stout 25 years of crossing and recrossing to produce. Also on display are all the past winners of the annual Stout Medal, the American Hemerocallis Society's highest award. Across the road from the day lily collection is the Ruth Rea Howell Family Garden, a focal point of NYBG's programs for kids.

THE NEW YORK BOTANICAL GARDEN,
BRONX

23

More gardens near the Conservatory provide inspiration for amateurs seeking new ideas. The Jane Watson Irwin Perennial Garden shows off many handsome varieties suited for home use. Next to the Irwin garden are the Totemeier Iris Collection; the Nancy Bryan Luce Herb Garden, illustrating traditional uses of herbs for fragrances, flavors, medicines, and dyes; and the small Chemurgic Garden, featuring plants of economic significance. At the opposite end of the Conservatory, a great favorite with visitors are the seasonal borders, which display 80 kinds of tulips in spring, followed by notable varieties of annuals, including cleomes, begonias, impatiens, zinnias, and marigolds.

An adjoining area is devoted to five Demonstration Gardens, installed to provide ideas for home use. Across the way from the Demonstration Gardens are beds of peonies with showy, fragrant blooms, and a curving walk bordered by 160 daffodil cultivars, interplanted with an equal variety of day lilies to provide color from early spring through fall.

❖ THE NEW YORK BOTANICAL GARDEN, 200th Street and Southern Boulevard, Bronx, NY 10458-5126. Tel. (718) 817-8700 (information) or 817-8577 (group tours). **Facilities**: Visitor information center and gift shop in the Museum Building; snacks and lunches at the Tulip Tree Café outside, and at the Snuff Mill River Terrace Café across the river. Picnic areas at the Snuff Mill and Twin Lakes. Rest rooms and telephones in major buildings. Generally accessible to the handicapped. Cars must be parked in lots near the entrance; trams take passengers on regular tours of the grounds. No pets allowed. **Open**: Tuesday through Sunday year-round, except New York City holidays, 10 a.m. to 6 p.m., April through October; 10 a.m. to 4 p.m., November through March. Admission charged. **Directions**: By car, follow signs on Pelham, Bronx River, or Henry Hudson parkways. By train, the Garden is 20 minutes from Grand Central Station. Take the Harlem line to the Botanical Garden station. A special NYBG shuttle bus also operates on Saturdays and Sundays from Manhattan; for information and reservations, call (718) 817-8700.

The grand Museum Building, built in 1901, features a heroic fountain and huge floral banners. Below: A partial view of the Thomas H. Everett Rock Garden, where close to 1,000 species and varieties illustrate the use of plants in different habitats.

❖

WAVE HILL, BRONX

A flower-decked pergola provides a spot from which to view the Palisades across the Hudson River. Opposite: Evergreen conifers highlight the winding paths of the Wild Garden.

Whether you're a serious gardener looking for new ideas or someone who just likes flowers and fresh air, Wave Hill is not to be missed. This former estate high above the Hudson has something for everyone, including an array of outstanding gardens as well as programs in horticulture and the visual and performing arts.

From the early nineteenth century, Wave Hill's panoramic site has been enjoyed by a succession of residents, including jurist William Lewis Morris, who built a country villa there in 1843; publisher William Henry

WAVE HILL, BRONX

Appleton, who bought the property as a summer home in 1866; and, at one time or another, such luminaries as Arturo Toscanini, Teddy Roosevelt, and Samuel Clemens, a.k.a. Mark Twain.

In 1893, George W. Perkins, an associate of financier J. P. Morgan, acquired Wave Hill. With the help of a landscape gardener from Vienna, Albert Millard, he and his wife improved the grounds with gardens, greenhouses, and, above a recreation building buried in the hillside, a colonnade framing a spectacular view of the Palisades (which Perkins helped to preserve).

The gardens today reflect the prodigious talents of Marco Polo Stufano, Wave Hill's director of horticulture since 1967, and John Nally, who joined the staff in 1970 and served as curator of gardens until his death in 1988. Rather than settle for a series of didactic plant collections like some public institutions, they tried to preserve the flavor of a private, personal garden tended by enthusiastic and knowledgeable amateurs—a place where other amateurs could not only come to enjoy themselves but discover new ideas to take home.

Every year Stufano and his staff of seven gardeners comb seed catalogues and other sources to find fresh varieties that they can experiment with and share with visitors. Interpretive gardener Madeleine Keeve points out that new plants are apt to come from almost anywhere, be it a famous British garden or a humble tire planter on a Yonkers street. A few years ago, she recalls, Stufano and Nally were waiting for a bus in downtown Chicago when the latter spotted an unusually beautiful aster sprouting from a sidewalk crack. While a bus driver eyed them in disbelief, they carefully pried out their find to bring back to Wave Hill, where it was planted in the Wild Garden as *Aster ericoidies* 'Chicago Bus Stop', much to the delight of their fans.

To most visitors, the triumph of Stufano and co. is the exuberant, old-fashioned Flower Garden, which occupies a place of honor inside the entrance on the right. Here something is in bloom from March through November, with a feast of color during the summer months. Among beds filled with clematis, hydrangeas, irises, peonies, roses, and other plantings—many of them old varieties from the Perkinses' time—brick paths converge on a small center "stage" where potted plants of seasonal and special interest are displayed.

An elegant backdrop for the Flower Garden is provided by the Perkinses' Victorian-style greenhouses, which are entered through a central Palm House filled with the heady perfume of white-flowering winter jasmine as well as the blooms of yellow allamandas, blue-flowering plumbago, and golden mimosa. To the left a Tropical House contains a dazzling range of warm-climate species; succulents from arid regions are displayed in a Cactus House to the right.

Behind the greenhouses, visitors ascend through a terraced Herb Garden, nicely enclosed by the foundation walls of other greenhouses now defunct. Here close to 100 kinds of herbs are grown, from Egyptian onion to dittany of Crete, including many unusual species that are labeled with their lore and uses, and which visitors are encouraged to touch, feel, and smell. At the top of the garden is the Thomas H. Everett Alpine Greenhouse, where a rare public collection of mountain gems like lewisias, primulas, and drabas can be viewed through the windows as they come into bloom.

Still farther up the slope is the Wild Garden, a naturalistic, richly textured landscape in the English tradition that combines plantings of native species from around the world, punctuated by the twisting trunks of cutleaf staghorn sumacs and soft clouds of yews.

The last stop is the Aquatic Garden, where a central pool shows off tropical and hardy water lilies, lotus, papyrus, taro, and other aquatic plants. Around the garden are arbors covered with silver lace and other flowering vines. At one end is a striking and relatively new addition: a monocot border of tall, waving ornamental grasses and bold-flowered cannas, set off in summer by tubbed palms, New Zealand phormiums, and banana plants.

One of the nicest things about the place is that each year there are more improvements, and a few surprises, for Wave Hill's loyal clientele. "Static" is one word Marco Polo Stufano doesn't recognize. "The art of a garden is in doing it," he says. "A garden should never be 'done.' "

❖ WAVE HILL, 675 West 252nd Street, Bronx, NY 10471. Tel. (718) 549-3200. **Facilities**: Sitting areas overlooking the Hudson, gift shop, picnic area, a small café offering beverages and snacks, rest rooms. The main grounds and flower garden are accessible to visitors with disabilities; the upper gardens have steps and gravel paths. **Open**: Six days a week, Tuesday through Sunday, year-round, 9 a.m. to 4:30 p.m.; extended to 5:30 p.m. and dusk on Wednesdays, from mid-May to mid-October. Greenhouses open from 10 a.m. to 12 noon and 2 p.m. to 4 p.m. Closed New Year's Day and Christmas. Admission free on weekdays. There is a charge on weekends and holidays. **Directions**: From the south, take the Henry Hudson Parkway north to the 246-250th Street exit and follow Wave Hill signs; from the north, Henry Hudson Parkway south to 254th Street exit and follow signs. By train, take the Hudson line to the Riverdale station. By bus, take the Manhattan-Riverdale express bus (212-652-8400) to 252nd Street. By Mosholu Limousine vans (718-543-6900), go to Wave Hill gate. By subway, take the IND 1/9 subway to 231st Street connecting with Bx 7/10/24 bus to 252nd Street.

L O W E R   H U D S O N   E A S T

T H E   D O N A L D   M . K E N D A L L   S C U L P T U R E G A R D E N S   A T   P E P S I C O , P U R C H A S E

The Ornamental Grass Garden shows off some 40 varieties of grasses and sedges. They are of different shapes and textures, some striped or variegated, others beautifully tinted in fall.

Of all the man-made landscapes in the Hudson Valley region, the most arrestingly contemporary—and one of the most richly rewarding—is the Donald M. Kendall Sculpture Gardens at PepsiCo's World Headquarters, located a few miles east of White Plains. Here horticulture, sculpture, and architecture are melded to create a unique series of visual experiences, not only

THE DONALD M. KENDALL SCULPTURE
GARDENS, PURCHASE

Opposite, from the top:
Among the modern sculptures
highlighting the Golden Path
is the realistic Three People
on Four Benches, *done by*
George Segal in 1979.
In the background is the
geometrically planted Birch
Grove. Below right: Alexander
Calder's Hats Off, *done in*
1969. Below left: Across
the lake, with its flocks of
ducks and geese, rises
Henry Moore's bronze
Double Oval *of 1967.*

for employees but for visitors, who are welcome to enjoy the 112 acres of gardens any day of the year.

This modern corporate Versailles had its genesis in 1965, when the Pepsi-Cola Company decided to move its headquarters from Manhattan to greener suburban pastures once used by the Blind Brook Polo Club. To reinforce the image of a forward-looking corporation, Donald Kendall, then PepsiCo's chairman and chief executive officer, began purchasing modern sculptures for the grounds, personally choosing and supervising the installation of each. Over a quarter century the collection has grown to more than 40 pieces by major international artists, ranging from Auguste Rodin's life-size bronze *Eve,* created in 1881, to Robert Davidson's towering *Totems,* completed in 1986.

Much of PepsiCo's astounding beauty today, however, is attributable to the late, great English landscape designer Russell Page, whom Kendall commissioned in 1981 to connect the sculptures, grounds, and buildings into a coherent, dramatic whole. Page's first stroke of genius was to install a "Golden Path," a ribbon of honey-colored gravel that loops around the grounds, inviting visitors to contemplate individual sculptures and to explore new gardens designed by Page himself.

Don Kendall fondly recalls the aging master scooting about in a golf cart, directing assistants to mark with stakes the precise location of each new tree and shrub. In some places the plantings were selected to frame and enhance the sculptures; in others they were massed as living sculptures in themselves. PepsiCo was Russell Page's last, and finest, public work of art. He died in 1985.

An outing at PepsiCo—which may take from a couple of hours to all day, including a picnic by the lake—can be enjoyed at any season (it is striking even in winter, when the basic structures of sculpture and plantings are revealed against the sky and snow).

An exuberant greeting is provided by Alexander Calder's three-story stabile *Hats Off,* its steel plates of fire-engine red contrasted against a backdrop of blue spruce. Stroll north, past other monumental sculptures by Dubuffet, Pomodoro, and Rodin, then through glorious ornamental plantings of rhododendrons, azaleas, roses, and other flowering shrubs.

A detour here (or on the way back) takes you into the headquarters'

courtyard gardens, which are landscaped on a more formal, intimate scale. At the center is David Wynne's graceful fountain piece, *Girl with a Dolphin*. Other sculptures adorn sunken courts on either side, and a charming pool below the main entrance is surrounded by pleached lindens and enlivened with willow trees, floral islands, and pulsing water jets.

Along the Golden Path to the north are gardens that Page created on different themes. One is the Birch Grove, a collection of 13 kinds of birches planted in geometric patterns, their silvery trunks accented by a carpet of blue grape hyacinths in spring. Nearby is the Gold Garden, a stunning tour de force featuring banked specimens of all descriptions, evergreen and deciduous, whose leaves are naturally variegated or tinged with gold. Beyond the entrance road to the west is the Stream Garden, where a side trail winds through ferns, hostas, astilbes, lobelias, trilliums, anemones, and other plants that thrive in moisture and shade. An outstanding attraction at any season is the Ornamental Grass Garden, where the mounded foliage and flower plumes of some 40 types of grasses and sedges wave softly in the breeze.

Below a corner of the headquarters building, beyond a collection of flowering crab apples, magnolias, and cherries, is the largest, and probably the most popular, of the gardens that Page designed: the Perennial Border and Water Lily Pools. Here a pavilion in classic English style looks out over a subtle geometry of water, islands, and bridges planted with hardy and tropical water lilies, lotuses, irises, and other aquatic plants. Against the hillside is a long bank of perennials. Defining the garden on the open side are a formal allée of 'Mount Fuji' cherries and a covey of topiary yews.

From here the Golden Path winds down to and around the lake, with side trips into a woodland garden of sweetly scented deciduous azaleas and a North American wild flower trail. Near the end of the loop, a pleasant picnic grove overlooks the willow-bordered lake, whose tall, jetting fountain and abundant waterfowl make it a favorite of employees and visitors alike.

❖ THE DONALD M. KENDALL SCULPTURE GARDENS AT PEPSICO WORLD HEADQUARTERS, 700 Anderson Hill Rd., Purchase, NY 10577. Tel. (914) 253-2000. **Facilities**: Information center, picnic area by the lake, rest rooms. Free map guide. Acessible to the handicapped on hard gravel paths. **Open**: Daily from 9 a.m. to 5 p.m.; in summer open until dusk. Admission free. **Directions**: From the south, take the Hutchinson River Parkway north to Exit 28, left onto Lincoln Avenue and proceed north to second light; turn right onto Anderson Hill Road to PepsiCo entrance on the right. From the north, take Hutchinson River Parkway south to Exit 30, right on King Street (Rte. 120A), left on Anderson Hill Road to PepsiCo entrance on left. Inside the grounds, turn left at the intersection and follow Loop Road to the visitor parking lot and information center. By train, take the New Haven line to the Rye station and a taxi from there.

❖

SUNNYSIDE, TARRYTOWN

Daffodils cover a hillside in spring above Washington Irving's picturesque home, dubbed the "snuggery."

The earliest surviving example of the nineteenth century Romantic landscape movement in the Hudson Valley is Sunnyside, Washington Irving's famous home, where, as Irving once put it, "the useful and the beautiful in rural life are combined."

On entering the parking lot, don't miss the cutting garden on the right, which fairly bursts with tall sunflowers, hollyhocks, cosmos, cleomes, celosias, and other old-fashioned favorites; along with a small vegetable plot, it preserves the spirit of a large kitchen and flower garden that the owner once maintained on more than an acre here.

Down the hill from the reception center is the house itself. Originally the home of a tenant farmer on the vast Philips estate, the small stone cottage was bought by Irving in 1835, when he was 52 and had achieved world fame. (During the late eighteenth century the cottage had been owned by a branch of the Van Tassel family, whom Irving immortalized in "The Legend of Sleepy Hollow," along with "Rip Van Winkle," his best-known tale.)

With the help of a friend, painter George Harvey, Irving set about remodeling his "snuggery" with Dutch stepped gables and Gothic and Romanesque motifs, later adding a three-story tower he called The Pagoda to accommodate his frequent guests. The front entrance today is almost hidden by huge old wisteria vines, which bloom copiously each spring as they did in Irving's day. Below the house a stroll along a river path affords fine views north to the Tappan Zee at the Hudson's widest point.

Not only Sunnyside's eclectic architecture but its picturesque land-

SUNNYSIDE, TARRYTOWN

LOWER HUDSON EAST

scaping reflects Irving's love of international travel, including his stint as United States Minister to Spain in 1844–46. A notable feature is a lovely, tree-sheltered pond he created by damming a small stream—a romantic setting he referred to as his "little Mediterranean." In such surroundings Irving retired to write his final works, including a five-volume *Life of George Washington*, after whom he was named.

Irving descendants occupied Sunnyside until 1945, when John D. Rockefeller, Jr.'s Sleepy Hollow Restorations purchased the property and set about restoring it to its mid-nineteenth century charm. Along with other restorations featured in this book—Philipsburg Manor, Van Cortlandt Manor, and Montgomery Place—Sunnyside is now operated by a successor organization, Historic Hudson Valley.

❖ SUNNYSIDE, Rte. 9 in Tarrytown, NY, one mile south of the New York State Thruway. Administered by Historic Hudson Valley, 150 White Plains Road, Tarrytown, NY 10591. Tel. (914) 631-8200. **Facilities**: Reception center, gift shop, picnic area, rest rooms. Generally accessible to the handicapped, though some areas may prove difficult. For group tours and a calendar of events, call the number above. **Open**: Daily from 10 a.m. to 5 p.m.; closed Tuesdays, New Year's Day, Thanksgiving, and Christmas. Closed January and February. Admission charged. **Directions**: From the New York State Thruway (I-87), take Exit 9, Tarrytown, proceed south on Rte. 9 one mile and look for sign on right. By train, take the Hudson line to the Tarrytown station and a free shuttle bus from there. Metro-North Railroad also runs weekend tours of Sunnyside, Lyndhurst, and Philipsburg Manor from May 20 to October 29.

A footbridge leads over a stream below the pond, which is a romantic spot Irving called his "little Mediterranean."

SUNNYSIDE, TARRYTOWN

❖

LYNDHURST, TARRYTOWN

Five hundred bushes representing more than 100 varieties highlight the Rose Garden, introduced by Helen Gould. The pergola from her era was replaced by an elaborate cast-stone and wrought-iron gazebo.

If you'd like to savor a veritable arboretum of magnificent trees, composed around sweeping lawns in the manner of a noble English estate, Lyndhurst is the place.

Pick up a grounds map at the gate and savor the specimens as you go: larches, camperdown elms, gingkos, lindens, copper beeches, European weeping beeches, Ohio chestnuts, Norway spruces, and more, plus a host of smaller flowering species like magnolias, dogwoods, mock oranges, lilacs, weigelas, and rhododendrons.

Although Andrew Jackson Downing had no direct hand in the landscaping, his enthusiasm for the English Romantic tradition was clearly shared by his friend Alexander Jackson Davis, who designed the estate in 1838 as a retirement residence for William Paulding, a former mayor of New York City and a general in the War of 1812. (Downing was pleased with the results, writing Davis, "I have never seen anything to equal it.") In 1864 George Merritt, a New York merchant, bought the property and had Davis enlarge the house. He hired Ferdinand Mangold, Davis's own gardener, to expand the plantings as his resident landscapist, a role Mangold filled for many years. An avid amateur horticulturist, Merritt also constructed an immense greenhouse that, in addition to exotic plant collections, boasted a reception hall, a gymnasium, and a billiard room.

In 1880 Lyndhurst and its 67 acres were purchased by railroad

LYNDHURST, TARRYTOWN

magnate Jay Gould, but within months the wood-framed greenhouse was destroyed by fire. Gould immediately commissioned the firm of Lord & Burnham, in nearby Irvington, to rebuild it along new lines. The resulting structure, 376 feet long and 36 feet wide, was heralded as the largest privately owned greenhouse in the world, and one of the first in America to use cast-iron framing (it inspired similar Lord & Burnham conservatories erected for the public at The New York Botanical Garden, the Brooklyn Botanic Garden, and San Francisco's Golden Gate Park). Gould's glassy extravaganza housed a large orchid collection as well as azaleas, camellias, and ferns, plus ample supplies of fresh cut flowers for the mansion and Gould's Fifth Avenue house in Manhattan. In a service building behind were sleeping quarters for some of the gardening staff, which numbered more than 30 employees.

Following Gould's death in 1892, his daughter Helen lavished her own attentions on Lyndhurst, among other projects creating a circular rose garden just west of the greenhouse. The greenhouse itself, abandoned during World War II for lack of fuel, is now an eerie, glassless skeleton—a striking relic of America's Gilded Age. Helen's garden, however, still flourishes with more than a hundred varieties of roses, from prize-winning modern hybrids to some of the old-fashioned species she loved so well. The Garden Club of Irvington-on-Hudson tends the Rose Garden as its year-round project.

❖ LYNDHURST, 635 South Broadway, Tarrytown, NY 10591. Tel. (914) 631-4481. Administered by the National Trust for Historic Preservation. **Facilities**: The 1865 Carriage House contains a museum gallery, gift shop, and Carriage House Cafe for lunch from 10 a.m. to 3 p.m. Thursday through Sunday, May through October. Group tours and special annual events. The grounds are generally accessible to the handicapped, but those needing assistance to tour the mansion should call ahead. **Open**: May through October, daily, 10 a.m. to 5 p.m.; November through April, weekends only, 10 a.m. to 5 p.m. Closed New Year's Day, Thanksgiving, and Christmas. Open at other times to groups of 10 or more by advance reservation. Admission charged. **Directions**: By car, take the New York State Thruway (I-87) to Exit 9, Tarrytown,

go south on Rte. 9 one half mile and look for sign on right. By train, take the Hudson line to the Tarrytown station and a taxi from there. Metro-North Railroad runs weekend tours of Sunnyside, Lyndhurst, and Philipsburg Manor from May 20 to October 29.

Lyndhurst, surrounded by magnificent specimen trees, is one of America's finest Gothic Revival style mansions.

LYNDHURST, TARRYTOWN

PHILIPSBURG MANOR, NORTH TARRYTOWN

Opposite: A bridge leads across the dam which turns the Pocantico River into a mill pond. At left is the gristmill and granary, from which milled wheat and corn were shipped to Manhattan by boat. At right is the manor house, restored to its appearance in the early 1700s. To its right is the kitchen garden, used by the early Dutch settlers. Below: The opening blossoms of nasturtiums (Tropaeolum majus) adorn the kitchen garden. The plants were used in salads.

The culinary fare of the region's early Dutch settlers is brought to life in the large kitchen garden at Philipsburg Manor, which is planted with herbs and vegetables popular in the early 1700s. As such, it represents the oldest kind of garden in the Hudson Valley, a working affair that stands in sharp contrast with the ornate pleasure grounds of later estates.

Behind a low wooden fence, originally erected to keep out wandering livestock, visitors can stroll among raised rectangular beds edged with lavender and southernwood and displaying some 80 species in all. Planted nearest the old stone manor house are such staples as cucumbers and scarlet runner beans, as well as herbs used for flavoring and scent—basil, winter and summer savory, oregano, sage, spearmint, peppermint, lemon balm, licorice root, marjoram, lovage, rosemary, and thyme.

The central section is devoted to standbys of early cuisine: lettuce, cabbage, peas, spinach, carrots, beets, turnips, onions, leeks, peppers, parsnips, dill, coriander, skirrets, parsley, and chives. The far section of the garden shows off many of the plants used by the settlers for medicines, teas, dyes, and miscellaneous ends—horehound, catnip, foxglove, chamomile, wormwood, feverfew, sweet woodruff, costmary, comfrey, valerian, tansy, yarrow, soapwort, safflower, and elecampane, as well as teasel, lady's bedstraw, broom corn, tobacco, and flax.

Behind a nearby barn, where attendants in period costume tend sheep, goats, and oxen typical of an eighteenth-century farm, is an orchard planted with varieties of apple, pear, and cherry trees available in those days. Here, too, are bee skeps of the type that provided the settlers with honey for sweetening and wax for making candles and lubricating gears.

On the other side of the manor house, which is reached by a scenic bridge across a mill pond dam, is a reconstructed gristmill where corn and wheat from the Philips family's vast estate—originally a royal land grant of more than 50,000 acres—was once ground by slaves, stored in an adjoining granary, and shipped downriver to Manhattan from the manor's wharf.

The site of Philipsburg Manor, Upper Mills (the family once operated a Lower Mills in Yonkers) was acquired by John D. Rockefeller, Jr., around 1940. The 20 remaining acres and key buildings were subsequently restored to the period of the manor's greatest prosperity, 1720–50, and opened to the public in 1969.

❖ PHILIPSBURG MANOR, Rte. 9, North Tarrytown, NY. Administered by Historic Hudson Valley, 150 White Plains Road,

PHILIPSBURG MANOR, NORTH
TARRYTOWN

Tarrytown, NY 10591. Tel. (914) 631-8200. **Facilities**: Reception center, exhibits, gift shop, rest rooms. Picnic area overlooking the mill pond. Accessible to the handicapped. **Open**: Daily, 10 a.m. to 5 p.m.; closed Tuesdays, New Year's Day, Thanksgiving, and Christmas. Closed January and February. Admission charged. **Directions**: From the New York State Thruway (I-87), take Exit 9, Tarrytown, then Rte. 119 to Rte. 9 and go north two miles. The entrance to Philipsburg Manor is on the left. Or take the Saw Mill River Parkway to Rte. 287, then follow Rte. 119 to Rte. 9. By train, take the Hudson line to the Tarrytown station and take a taxi or bus service to Philipsburg Manor; some routes include a stop at Philipse Manor, which is even closer. Metro-North Railroad runs weekend tours of Sunnyside, Lyndhurst, and Philipsburg Manor from May 20 to October 29.

❖

KYKUIT,
POCANTICO HILLS

The entrance to the mansion at Kykuit, with wisteria vines climbing in between the windows. The imposing Georgian facade is surmounted by a pediment containing sculptures by Tonetti.

When John D. Rockefeller, Sr., began quietly buying up land east of Tarrytown in the early 1890s, he envisioned a simple country retreat where he could enjoy the fresh air and scenery, which reminded him of his rural origins in upstate New York.

Others, however, had different ideas of what befitted America's richest man. Lesser luminaries were already turning the riverfront into a millionaires' row. The editor of the *Tarrytown Argus* confidently predicted that John D. would build a "regal castle," no expenses spared.

By the fall of 1893, Rockefeller had acquired some 400 acres—his holdings would eventually grow to 3,500 acres in 80 separate purchases—and with his wife, Laura, had moved into a modest Victorian house previously built on the site. It stood 300 yards below a rocky hilltop, named Kykuit after the earlier Dutch settlers' word for "lookout."

The prospect from Kykuit was, and is, one of the most breathtaking on the Hudson, sweeping more than 50 miles from West Point on the north, over the river's widest point at the Tappan Zee, and southward to Grant's Tomb and the skyscrapers of New York. The new owner was so entranced that he built an observation tower on the summit just to savor the view.

In 1902 their wooden home was destroyed by fire, and the Rockefellers were forced to move to another house on the grounds, one without the view. At this point their son and heir John D., Jr., who had been given the responsibility of helping develop the estate, saw a chance

KYKUIT, POCANTICO HILLS

A decorative colonnade and a grand three-tiered fountain set off the rose garden at Kykuit.

to please his father and at the same time bring his own dreams to life. He approached the architectural firm of Delano and Aldrich, who drew up plans for Kykuit II, a new house at the top of the summit—a peak-roofed stone lodge in late Victorian style thought to be unpretentious enough to suit his father's taste.

Despite John D., Senior's reservations that even this scheme was too big, work on the house began in 1906, with Junior in charge while his parents were largely away. When she finally saw it, however, the result was not to Laura Rockefeller's liking. At her request, new plans were drawn to rebuild the mansion in Georgian style with larger guest rooms, a new fourth floor for servants, and a more imposing main facade.

The guiding light of the renovation—and of the magnificent formal

LOWER HUDSON EAST

gardens that gradually materialized around the house—was William Welles Bosworth. Under Bosworth's and Junior's direction, work proceeded on Kykuit III. Ledgerock was blasted for terraces, fountains, and pools; water was piped in from reservoirs constructed on neighboring heights. Countless wagon loads of topsoil were hauled up switchback roads to make the barren summit bloom. Giant elms were transplanted to frame vistas; 200-year-old orange trees in tubs were imported from France (housing them in winter required a large Orangerie elsewhere on the grounds—which, of course, Bosworth also designed).

As a fitting entrance to the new mansion, a great forecourt was built on concrete coffering over the brow of the hill and flanked by towering wrought-iron gates with intricate floral patterns and the monogram JDR.

Conically trimmed evergreens accent a garden in the Italian villa style. At center is a statue by sculptor Aristide Maillol, Bather Putting Up Her Hair.

KYKUIT, POCANTICO HILLS

The court's focal point was an astonishing fountain sculpture nearly 40 feet high. A copy of the Oceanus Fountain in Florence's Boboli Gardens, its bowl was fashioned from a single piece of granite, weighed 37 tons, and had to be shipped up the Hudson, placed on rollers for the cross-country journey, and wrestled into place by steam winch and crane.

Around the house Bosworth created a series of terraced landscapes in the popular Italian villa style, with exuberant dashes of French and English thrown in. On one side was a semicircular rose garden; on the other, an enclosed, sunken garden, plus a boxed linden allée, a circular temple with a statue of Aphrodite as well as assorted grottoes, pavilions, and summer houses where the owners and their guests could tarry to enjoy a cup of tea or admire a view.

Surrounding the whole was the feature that John D. really loved: a private nine-hole golf course, which he played every day, rain or shine, and whose broad, lawnlike fairways not only provided a parklike English setting for the house but were forgiving of errant shots. A longtime Rockefeller employee, Tom Pyle, recalled that the only jarring note in "Mr. Senior's personal playground" was the Putnam Division of the New York Central Railroad, whose coal-fired trains occasionally belched soot and cinders on the immaculate white shirts of his golfing guests. John D. soon took care of the situation: he made a deal with the railroad to move their tracks five miles to the east.

The senior Rockefellers enjoyed driving about their far-flung domain on a network of carriage roads and trails that they had cut through the woods, and that would eventually total 75 miles (in 1983, the family donated some 750 acres at the northern edge of the property to the public as Rockefeller State Park). After John D.'s death in 1937, Junior and his wife, Abby, moved into the main house, where they raised a daughter and five famous sons, four of whom would eventually live in their own houses on the estate.

One of them, former New York Governor and U.S. Vice President Nelson A. Rockefeller, took up residence in Kykuit in 1963 and lived there with his family until his death in 1979. To the Rockefellers' earlier traditions as art patrons Nelson added his own special enthusiasm for modern art, building a series of underground galleries to house works by such artists as Warhol, Motherwell, Braque, Picasso, and Toulouse-Lautrec.

It is in the outdoor sculpture collection, however, that the range of styles and periods at Kykuit is most strikingly displayed. Here, against a backdrop recalling classical eras, are figures by leading twentieth-century sculptors—Brancusi, Noguchi, Giacometti, Calder, Moore, Nadelman, Nevelson, Nagare, Lipchitz, Liberman, Pomodoro, Arp, Maillol, Lachaise, and more.

❖ KYKUIT, Pocantico Hills, NY (North Tarrytown). Tel. (914) 631-9491. Administered by the Rockefeller Brothers Fund in cooperation with the National Trust for Historic Preservation. Tours by Historic Hudson Valley, 150 White Plains Road, Tarrytown, NY 10591. **Facilities:** Rest rooms. Generally accessible to the handicapped. **Open:** By small, pre-arranged tours only, leaving from Philipsburg Manor in nearby North Tarrytown. (Admission charged; see directions under Philipsburg Manor). For hours and reservations, contact Historic Hudson Valley at the address and number above. Individual visits to Kykuit are not permitted. For a seven-hour Hudson River cruise and guided Kykuit tour offered by New York Waterway, call (800) 533-3779. Metro-North Railroad runs weekend tours of Kykuit from May 20 to October 29; for information, call (914) 631-8200, ext. 615.

❖

VAN CORTLANDT MANOR, CROTON-ON-HUDSON

The outstanding feature of this early Dutch estate, which has been restored to its appearance between 1790 and 1814, is the "Long Walk," a brick path bordered by gardens and orchards typical of the day. The path links the Manor House, whose elegant wooden verandas were added to an older stone building around 1750, with the Ferry House, where stagecoach passengers on the old Albany Post Road once stopped for food and lodging before crossing the Croton River on an open barge. Along with other outbuildings, which included tenant houses, a gristmill, a sawmill, a church, and a school, they were once the center of an 86,000-acre private empire founded by Stephanus Van Cortlandt, the son of a soldier who arrived in New Amsterdam with the West India Company in 1638.

Starting at the Ferry House, visitors stroll between lines of lilacs and apple trees that are heavy with blossoms in spring, when bright beds of daffodils, tulips, and hyacinths are also in bloom. Above the walk is an orchard displaying varieties of apples, peaches, and pears that the Van Cortlandt family grew, and whose fruits are used in cooking demonstrations in the manor house.

Below the walk is a large kitchen garden planted with the kinds of vegetables and herbs that supplied the manor's residents and guests, including squashes, pumpkins, and scarlet runner beans. Adjacent is a rose garden.

At almost any season the Long Walk is a floral treat, boasting a hundred or more species of flowering plants, including many old-fashioned favorites like love-lies-bleeding and cockscomb.

❖ VAN CORTLANDT MANOR, Rte. 9, Croton-on-Hudson, NY 10520. Administered by Historic Hudson Valley, 150 White Plains Rd., Tarrytown, NY 10591. Tel. (914) 631-8200. **Facilities**: Reception center, gift shop, rest rooms. Picnic ground overlooking the Croton River. Accessible to the handicapped. **Open**: Daily, 10 a.m. to 5 p.m.; closed Tuesdays and New Year's Day, Thanksgiving, and Christmas. Closed January through March. Admission charged. **Directions**: From the New York State Thruway (I-87), take Exit 9, Tarrytown, go north on Rte. 9 for 11 miles and follow signs. By train, take the Hudson line to the Croton-Harmon station.

The Long Walk is bordered by a wealth of perennials, including several kinds of tulips in spring. At left are the prickly heads of teasel (Dipsacus sylvestris), an old-fashioned herb whose comblike texture was once used by weavers to raise, or tease, wool pile.

VAN CORTLANDT MANOR,
CROTON-ON-HUDSON

CARAMOOR, KATONAH

The June-blooming flowers of mountain laurel are a great popular favorite at Caramoor and elsewhere in the woodlands and gardens of the Hudson Valley.

For the last five decades Caramoor has been renowned for its summer concerts, once described by *The New York Times* as "the most stylish and civilized music festival in the nation." But whether you go there for a performance or not, plan on an hour or so to stroll the lavishly landscaped grounds of this 100-acre showpiece built during the 1930s by Walter Tower Rosen, a prominent New York lawyer, and his elegant wife, the former Lucie Bigelow Dodge.

The Rosens were passionate art lovers and musicians (he was a pianist; she played the violin). Their Spanish-style mansion, designed around a large Spanish Courtyard and a vast music room, became a repository for their collections of fine art as well as a setting for lively musical evenings that enchanted their friends. Recitals in the courtyard were first opened to the public in 1946, and were supplemented by larger concerts in a canopied Venetian Theater built in 1958. Following Mrs. Rosen's death a decade later, the house and grounds became an indoor-outdoor museum for all to enjoy.

A good way to sample Caramoor's pleasures is to start at the mansion courtyard, where a central fountain is set off by tulips, irises, astilbes, canna lilies, and other seasonal blooms. Cross the driveway, where a large Oriental-looking dovecote is surrounded by a "Sense Circle" of species appealing to all the senses (in keeping with Caramoor's desire to offer music, art, and garden experiences to the visually impaired, the handicapped, and the elderly). Proceed to the Tapestry Hedge, where densely planted evergreens form an imposing wall of sculpted shapes, and on to the picnic grounds and Italian Pavilion.

To the left of the pavilion, beginning at a small Victorian temple of love, is a series of garden vistas in which the Rosens took special delight. Here a path leads up the Cedar Walk, a shady grove with ferns and

rhododendrons that forms a dramatic approach to a walled garden, which is glimpsed mysteriously through a stone Veronese arch.

Inside the walled garden, among more cedars and ferns, is an unusual mound topped by a semicircular stone bench—a feature patterned after vantage points where medieval lords and ladies could tarry to look over their castle walls. The view in this case, however, is not out to a feudal domain, but down into a sunken garden filled with roses, perennials, and annuals. After descending into the sunken garden and coming out the other side, visitors can stroll past the main theater entrance with its central flower beds and ornate eighteenth-century Swiss iron gates, then past the Venetian Theater and back to the mansion parking lot.

CARAMOOR, KATONAH

An Oriental-looking dovecote is the focal point of a "Sense Circle," which has species chosen to appeal to all the senses, including smell.

On the way to or from Caramoor, try to stop at the nearby John Jay Homestead on Rte. 22, the early nineteenth-century farm of the former Governor of New York and Chief Justice of the United States, now a State Historic Site. Surrounded by hedges of lilac, privet, and cedar near the parking lot are formal gardens reflecting the tastes of five generations of the Jay family. Completed in 1983 under the direction of the Bedford Garden Club, they include a lower fountain garden with ornamental crab apples and an upper garden laid out around a sundial with cosmos, cleomes, snapdragons, and other flowers in circular beds.

❖ CARAMOOR CENTER FOR MUSIC AND THE ARTS, Girdle Ridge Road, Katonah, NY 10536. Tel. (914) 232-5035. **Facilities**: Museum

shop, garden shop, picnic areas, rest rooms. Concerts in June, July, and August. Generally accessible to the handicapped. **Open**: The grounds are open Wednesday through Sunday, 10 a.m. to 5 p.m., May through November. The museum is open Wednesday through Sunday, 1 p.m. to 4 p.m. Admission charged. **Directions**: From I-684/Saw Mill River Parkway take Exit 6 (Katonah-Cross River), go east on Rte. 35 to first stoplight, turn right on Rte. 22 to Girdle Ridge Rd. (1.9 miles) and follow signs to Caramoor gates one half mile on right. By train, take the Harlem line to the Katonah station and a taxi from there. To stop at the nearby John Jay Homestead and its gardens, return to Rte. 22 north and look for a sign on the right. The grounds are open year-round at no admission charge. For information, call (914) 232-5651.

One of the many garden features of Caramoor is a walled Sunken Garden, which is filled with roses, perennials, and annuals laid out in formal beds.

CARAMOOR, KATONAH

❖

MANITOGA, GARRISON

A woodland stream dances over rocks and down into a reflecting pool that owner Wright created out of an abandoned quarry hole.

Manitoga, an Algonquin word meaning "place of the great spirit," is a garden in a broader sense—a celebration of wild nature lovingly restored by man. Ian McHarg, a noted landscape architect, once wrote that it "may be the single superb example of ecological design in the United States. If it were in Japan, it would be a national monument."

When Russel Wright, the industrial designer, acquired the 80 acres in 1942 as a summer retreat, the site was sad to behold, the result of years of logging and quarrying and the ensuing dense, scraggly second growth. For three decades until his death in 1976, Wright labored to return the land to its original grace, at the same time carefully dramatizing key elements so that he and his guests could enjoy them even more.

He cleared underbrush, pruned limbs and cut a network of trails that followed the terrain's natural contours, highlighting "discoveries" along the way that range from secret alcoves of woodland wild flowers to breathtaking glimpses of the Hudson below. Overlooking the abandoned granite quarry Wright built a house he called Dragon Rock, fitting it into the stone of a cliff and redirecting a stream to cascade over nearby boulders into a reflecting pool formed in the quarry hole.

The land and house, originally bequeathed by their owner to The Nature Conservancy, were taken over in 1984 by a nonprofit corporation, Manitoga, Inc., among whose trustees were many of Wright's old friends. Today his forest garden—which connects with the Appalachian Trail and Hudson Highlands State Park to form a model "greenway"—is open to all nature lovers, who can hike through groves of ferns, tunnels of blooming mountain laurel, and fields of wild flowers, stopping for a quiet picnic at a wilderness spot like Deer Pool or Lost Pond.

Russel Wright became famous for designing beautiful objects for daily living, but he considered Manitoga his crowning achievement. His goal,

M A N I T O G A ,   G A R R I S O N

Part of the magic of Manitoga is a proliferation of ferns, here interplanted with wild flowers.

he wrote, was "to help people experience the wonder of nature in a new and intensely personal way." Thanks to him that is possible, for in the streams and leaves of his forest, only 40 miles from New York City, Manitoga's great spirit indeed lives on.

❖ **MANITOGA,** Rte. 9D, Garrison, NY 10524. Tel. (914) 424-3812. **Facilities**: A small "Guide House" with displays, maps, gifts, and rest rooms. Walking trails are difficult for the handicapped. **Open**: 9 a.m. to 4 p.m., Monday through Friday; 10 a.m. to 6 p.m. on weekends, April through October. Modest admission fee suggested. **Directions**: For a quick, scenic route from the south, take the Palisades Interstate Parkway, cross the Hudson on the Bear Mountain Bridge and head north on Rte. 9D for 2 miles; Manitoga's entrance is on the right. (Alternate: from Peekskill, take Rte. 6-202 to 9D). From the north, take Rte. 9D south from Cold Spring for 4 miles and look for the entrance on the left. By train, take the Hudson line to the Garrison station and a taxi from there.

❖

BOSCOBEL RESTORATION, GARRISON

In 1804 States Morris Dyckman, a descendant of an early Dutch settler, began building a handsome home in New York Federal style above the river at Montrose, naming it after Boscobel House in Shropshire, England. Dyckman died before the house was finished, leaving it to his young wife, Elizabeth. Over the years the property went through a series of family members and other owners until the Veterans Administration purchased it as a location for a hospital in 1945.

A decade later, finding no use for the mansion, the U.S. government sold it to a housewrecker for $35. Fortunately, an organization of admirers stepped in and managed to save the mansion, moving it to a new 35-acre site in Garrison, 15 miles north. Here, with support from Lila Acheson Wallace, cofounder of *The Reader's Digest*, Boscobel was rebuilt, restored, and opened to the public in 1961.

Visitors stop first at the Carriage House to buy admission tickets, look at displays, and join guided tours. From here a path leads through an apple orchard containing old-fashioned varieties like Northern Spy, Baldwin, and Cortlandt, whose blossoms put on a fine display in May and whose tasty fruits are sold in the gift shop each fall.

Down a small path to the right is the attractive Herb Garden, which is maintained by the Philipstown Garden Club. Here a central path, flanked by low espaliers of winter pear, leads to an Orangerie used to shelter tender plants during the colder months. On one side of the garden, four square beds with a bee skep in the center of each feature bright displays of tulips in spring; these are followed by rich tapestries of herbs. On the other side of the garden, more flower beds, each dominated by a flowering quince tree, center on an old-fashioned hand pump and trough.

The bright blooms of hollyhocks (Althaea rosea) are features of the Herb Garden at Boscobel.

LOWER HUDSON EAST

Perennial beds—featuring bee balm, iris, hollyhock, Chinese forget-me-not, Japanese anemone, dianthus, evening primrose, delphinium, lamb's ears, veronica, and yarrow—create a border for the entire garden.

The main walk continues to a formal rose garden, designed by Innocenti & Webel in a classic English wheel pattern and enclosed by a tall Carolina hemlock hedge. Here, around a central fountain, weeping cherry trees and tulips bloom in spring; they are followed in June by the flowering of 300 rose bushes, which include old varieties as well as modern hybrid tea roses.

An opening at the far end of the rose garden frames a splendid vignette of the Hudson, looking south over Constitution Island toward West Point and the rolling highlands beyond. For the full panorama, walk out across the lawn to a scenic overlook in front of the mansion. (The house itself is worth a guided tour: a showcase of decorative arts in the New York Federal style, it includes pieces by Duncan Phyfe and other leading New York cabinetmakers, as well as the Dyckmans' collection of English china and silver.)

A stroll around the grounds reveals other points of interest, among them an old springhouse and a "necessary house" whose sociable interior boasts no less than five seats. At the rear of the mansion, a long driveway flanked by maples leads to an entrance courtyard with more maples in the center and climbing hydrangeas on the walls. Bordering the drive are a wild flower meadow and daffodils around a pretty pond with a tall fountain jet. Boscobel's well-mannered air of welcome extends to its entrance and even its parking lot, which is nicely softened with tall hedges, pines, and dogwoods in a semicircular design.

❖ BOSCOBEL RESTORATION, INC., Garrison-on-Hudson, NY 10524. Tel. (914) 265-3638. **Facilities**: Gift shop, rest rooms. Events include productions of Shakespeare plays in July and August, exhibitions, workshops, and Christmas candlelight tours. **Open**: Daily, except Tuesdays, Thanksgiving, and Christmas; closed January and February. Hours: 10 a.m. to 5 p.m., April through October; 10 a.m. to 4 p.m., November, December, and March. Admission charged. **Directions**: From the south, take Rte. 9 to Rte. 403 to Rte. 9D and proceed north

An aerial view of Boscobel, surrounded by forest and fields. The gardens are at left, the mansion at right.

3.5 miles. From the north, New York Thruway south to I-84, east to Rte. 9D and south to Boscobel; or Taconic Parkway south to Rte. 301, west to Cold Spring and south on Rte. 9D. By train, take the Hudson line to the Garrison station and a taxi from there.

Opposite: An array of daffodils and birch trees by the side of a decorative pond. Left: The Herb Garden, which is divided into four beds with a bee skep at the center of each.

BOSCOBEL RESTORATION, GARRISON

❖

L O C U S T   G R O V E ,
P O U G H K E E P S I E

Samuel F. B. Morse, a leading nineteenth-century artist better known as the inventor of the telegraph, purchased a hundred acres just south of Poughkeepsie as his country home in the summer of 1847. The property was originally part of a larger farm estate developed in the late 1700s by one of the Livingston family, Henry, Jr., who named it Locust Grove after the tall black locusts that once lined his entrance drive. Morse hired architect Alexander Jackson Davis, a friend, to help him remodel and enlarge a Federal-style house built by a subsequent owner, John Montgomery, making it over in Italian villa style and landscaping the grounds to reflect newly popular concepts of Romantic design.

Morse, an early champion of landscape as a fine art, believed that the designer's "main object is to select from Nature all that is agreeable, and to reject or change everything that is disagreeable." He also believed in the healthy virtues of farming for both himself and his sons, devoting outlying areas to orchards, vegetable gardens, and the raising of livestock.

In 1901 Locust Grove was sold by Morse's heirs to William Young, a wealthy New York lawyer, who with his wife, Martha, maintained their illustrious predecessor's heritage while adding a few touches of their own. Before her death in 1975, their daughter Annette endowed a trust to maintain Locust Grove as a historic site open to the public, and to develop a large area of woodlands below the bluff, between the house and the river, as a wildlife sanctuary with scenic trails.

The approach to the house, like others of its era, is a long, curving drive through a parklike area of lawn dotted with specimen trees, among them a magnificent copper beech, a ginkgo, and a cut-leaf beech. Centered on the entrance, where the driveway passes under a porte-cochère fronted by two tall larches and a boxwood hedge, is a circular Victorian bed with a cast-iron pedestal and planting urn. On the south side of the mansion, a covered sitting porch wrapped in wisteria looks out under two immense sugar maples to the "French Garden," a parterre of colorful annuals around another urn.

Near the front of the property, partially enclosed by a decorative shrub border and a gardener's cottage now used as site headquarters, a large ornamental garden developed by the Youngs has been restored. A "ribbon" garden of the type popular around the turn of the century, it dis-

Samuel Morse remodeled his house in the Italian villa style, with a large arched porte-cochere in front. The grounds were handsomely landscaped to reflect concepts of Romantic design. A redbud blooms at right.

LOCUST GROVE, POUGHKEEPSIE

plays long beds of peonies, roses, irises, and other perennials, and, in one corner, a rustic sitting arbor entwined with actinidia vines.

❖ **LOCUST GROVE**, Young-Morse Historic Site, 370 South Rd., P.O. Box 1649, Poughkeepsie, NY 12601. Tel. (914) 454-4500. **Facilities**: Gift shop, rest rooms. For a schedule of tours, concerts and other events, call the number above. **Open**: Memorial Day weekend through September, Wednesday through Sunday, 10 a.m. to 4 p.m. Also open weekends in October and all Monday holidays. Groups and tours are welcome by reservation during April, May, October, November, and December. Admission to the grounds is free. **Directions**: Locust Grove is 2 miles south of the Mid-Hudson Bridge on Rte. 9 in Poughkeepsie. From the south, it is 10.8 miles north of I-84. By train, take the Hudson line to Poughkeepsie and a taxi from there.

VASSAR ARBORETUM, POUGHKEEPSIE

A massive London plane tree is one of the patriarchs among trees at the Vassar Arboretum.

Matthew Vassar, a prosperous Poughkeepsie brewer, wanted to do something for the society that helped make him a millionaire. At the urging of Milo Jewett, a local minister and educator, he settled on a novel scheme. He would found a female equivalent of Yale and Harvard—the first endowed women's college in the world.

Vassar tramped over several properties in Poughkeepsie, including a prominent one in clear view of dayboat passengers on the Hudson River

VASSAR ARBORETUM, POUGHKEEPSIE

The Shakespeare Garden features old roses, herbs, clematis, peonies, heathers, and other perennials.

bluffs. He finally opted for a 200-acre farm two miles inland, once the site of the Dutchess County racetrack, where his young ladies could enjoy the bounties of nature while less exposed to public scrutiny and the "immoral influences" of the city.

The land was scarce on trees when he purchased it, but Matthew Vassar was a landscaping enthusiast: he lived at Springside, a show-piece estate laid out for him by Andrew Jackson Downing a decade earlier. For four years he drove his carriage over to the site almost daily to check progress on "The College," later known as Main, a vast edifice designed by the celebrated architect James Renwick, Jr., in the French Second Empire style. Under a single roof nearly 500 feet long, it provided accommodations for 400 students and their teachers, plus classrooms and laboratories, a kitchen, a dining hall, a chapel, a laundry, and the first college art gallery in the United States.

In the summer of 1865, the founder was able to rejoice: "The building is ready, the park has been laid out and planted with shrubbery, shade trees and evergreens." That fall, Vassar College (the word "Female" was to be deleted in 1866 as "vulgar and offensive") welcomed 353 students for their first academic year. One of them, Martha Warner, wrote her mother: "I wish you could see old Mr. Vassar, his face is a perfect sunbeam; he seems entirely happy and contented to walk [around] and nod at all the girls. Every pleasant day his carriage is here."

Today Vassar has grown to 2,250 students, of both sexes, who enjoy a 1,000-acre campus that is noted not only for its architecture but for a veritable arboretum of more than 200 species of native and exotic trees. (A map of the Arboretum is available at the College's Message Center in Main Building.) Since 1868 it has been a tradition for each class to plant or choose its own tree and designate it with a plaque. Some classes gather under their trees at reunions in June to pay tribute to members who have died.

One of the most impressive specimens is a giant London plane tree between Main and the Library, which was adopted by the class of 1906. Others include the Class of 1973's big cucumber magnolia northeast of Main.

A stroll through the nobly shaded campus should include the Shakespeare Garden, which was laid out and planted in 1916 through the joint efforts of students of Shakespeare and botany, and later remodeled along the lines of a traditional English flower garden, with old roses, clematis, peonies, herbs, heathers, and other perennials. Above the garden rises another arboreal monarch, a white oak adopted by the Class of 1930, which is the oldest tree on campus.

"No better symbol for a college than a tree!" wrote Henry Noble MacCracken, Vassar's president from 1915 to 1946. "Matthew Vassar must have thought of this when he planted his trees and when he said that a college must be a living entity, having capacities of growth and of adaptability. And when a college, like a tree, is planted by the river of the water of life, whatever it doeth shall prosper."

❖ VASSAR COLLEGE, Poughkeepsie, NY 12601. Tel. (914) 437-7000. **Facilities**: Rest rooms in main buildings. Accessible to the handicapped. **Open**: Year-round. Admission free. **Directions**: From the Taconic State Parkway, take Rte. 44 or 55 to Poughkeepsie and look for Vassar College sign on left. From New York State Thruway Exit 18 (New Paltz), proceed east on Rte. 299 and south on Rte. 9W; follow Rte. 44/55 across the Mid-Hudson Bridge, continue for 2 miles and look for college sign. By train, take the Hudson line to Poughkeepsie and a taxi from there.

❖

ROOSEVELT HOMES: SPRINGWOOD AND VAL-KILL, HYDE PARK

On Sunday morning April 15, 1945, a long funeral train pulled into a siding below Springwood, the Roosevelts' riverfront estate at Hyde Park. As artillery on the hill fired a measured 21-gun salute and a formation of bombers flew overhead, Eleanor Roosevelt, Harry Truman, and other mourners accompanied the casket, winding slowly up the road through the forest her husband had loved, past the ice pond where he had swum, and the meadow he had sledded as a boy.

Six hundred West Point cadets led the procession into the large rose garden at the center of the grounds. Here the coffin was lowered into a grave. Riflemen fired three volleys; a bugler sounded taps. Franklin Delano Roosevelt was left at rest in his mother's rose garden, as he had wished. Seventeen years later his wife was to join him beside the same white marble monument, in her own myrtle-covered bed. On the other side, two small stones mark the graves of their favorite Scottie, Fala, and a German shepherd, Chief.

The setting is appropriate. The name Roosevelt, in fact, derives from the Dutch "field of roses," and the family crest bears three red roses on a shield. When Franklin's father, James, bought Springwood in 1867, he and his first wife, Rebecca, picked "thousands of roses before breakfast" from the same garden, which was then planted with fruit trees and vegetables as well. When his second wife, Sara, took over as Springwood's grande dame, she built a new greenhouse next to the garden to supply flowers for the mansion and removed the fruits and vegetables in favor of

flowers set off by panels of well-mown grass. Her love for roses in particular was impressed on her son, who considered the garden the most beautiful part of the estate and specificied that he be buried there.

Today thousands of people a year visit the graves, as well as the family mansion and the FDR Library and Museum nearby. The original hemlock hedge enclosing the garden, now well over a century old, forms a towering backdrop for 28 varieties of roses in separate beds—nearly 600 bushes in all, which along with borders of tulips, peonies, and annuals are designed to provide color from spring through fall. The roses range from older hybrid perpetuals like 'Jules Margotten' and the grandiflora 'Queen Elizabeth' to classic hybrid teas like 'Chrysler Imperial', 'Tropicana', 'Double Delight' and 'Peace'.

ROOSEVELT HOMES: SPRINGWOOD AND
VAL-KILL, HYDE PARK

❖

VAL-KILL

The Roosevelt penchant for flowers can also be seen at nearby Val-Kill, the rustic retreat that Eleanor Roosevelt made her personal home for nearly 40 years, and where she often entertained family and friends. Here, along the banks of a pretty, willow-bordered stream, Eleanor made it a daily ritual to walk through her woods and meadows, looking for the first snowdrops or dogwood blooms. From a small rose garden and a larger cutting garden, still maintained on the site, she cut roses, dahlias, peonies, and other blossoms to make arrangements for each guest's room. Visitors leaving Val-Kill often found farewell bouquets wrapped in damp paper and placed in their cars. Eleanor's love of flowers was simple and direct: "They carry a message of beauty which we can share the world over."

❖ HOME OF FRANKLIN D. ROOSEVELT NATIONAL HISTORIC SITE, Rte. 9, and ELEANOR ROOSEVELT NATIONAL HISTORIC SITE, Rte. 9G, administered by the National Park Service, 519 Albany Post Rd., Hyde Park, NY 12538. Tel. (914) 229-9115. **Facilities**: Visitor center, gift shop, FDR Library and Museum, picnic area, rest rooms. Generally accessible to the handicapped.**Open**: Grounds are open 9 a.m. to sundown year-round. Admission to the grounds is free. Admission is charged for the museum and mansion (the latter is closed Mondays and Tuesdays); visitors over 62 and under 16 are admitted free. Val-Kill is open Wednesday through Sunday, May through October, 9 a.m. to sundown, and on weekends only during November and December, March and April; closed January and February. Admission free. Both sites are closed New Year's Day, Thanksgiving, and Christmas. **Directions**: From Poughkeepsie (junction of routes 9 and 44/55), go 5 miles north on Rte. 9 and look for FDR home sign on left.

A map and directions to Val-Kill are available at the information/ticket booth. By train, take the Hudson line to Poughkeepsie and a taxi from there. Metro-North Railroad runs Saturday tours of the Roosevelt Homes and Vanderbilt Mansion from May 20 to October 28.

❖

VANDERBILT MANSION, HYDE PARK

When a local paper in 1895 carried the headline "Another Millionaire in Dutchess County," residents of Hyde Park were not especially impressed. Many of them already worked for, or sold goods or services to, the likes of John Jacob Astor, Jacob Ruppert, James Roosevelt, and Ogden Mills. The opulence of the Hudson aristocracy, awesome though it might be, was just another fact of life.

The Italian Renaissance-style mansion, seen here from one end, is set off by magnificent trees.

Gradually, however, it became apparent that Frederick William Vanderbilt, grandson of the railroading Commodore, was going to outdo them all. On 600 acres that he had acquired from Astor's grandson,

75

The Italian Gardens were laid out on several levels. A walk bordered by perennial beds leads to an arbor and a reflecting pool with a statue of a bathing maiden.

Walter Langdon, he commissioned McKim, Mead and White to design a 50-room palace of Indiana limestone in Italian Renaissance style, which would be furnished with art objects from around the world.

Outside, under Vanderbilt's critical eye, workmen labored to transform the grounds, laying out carriage drives, creating a miniature lake, building an elegant stone bridge across Crum Elbow Creek. To enhance the existing landscaping—much of it done for a previous owner, the distinguished physician-botanist David Hosack, by André Parmentier, one of the first professional landscapers in the U.S.—specimen trees were carefully preserved, new species were added, and the whole set off by acres of manicured lawns. As he did with his art objects, Vanderbilt took great pride in his collection of trees, which included European and American beeches, English elms, Norway spruces, and an immense ginkgo from China that remains one of the most impressive in the United States.

It was in the Italian Gardens south of the mansion, however, that Frederick William Vanderbilt outdid even himself. In 1902 he hired a landscape architect with the fortuitous name of James L. Greenleaf to redesign and enlarge the site of former gardens. Behind a gardener's cottage and a sizable tool house, the only older structures on the grounds that were saved, Greenleaf laid out plantings on eight terraced levels, framed by walls and piers of bold red brick.

On the upper level were erected a series of greenhouses for roses, palms, and other tender plants (the structures have since been torn down and replaced by lawns and flower beds). Two levels in the central section were given over to parterres of flowering annuals. The lower level was devoted to a long, formal walk flanked by cherry trees and raised beds faced with stone retaining walls. The beds today are planted with a variety of perennials, including wall cress, columbine, blue Virginia cowslip, mountain bluets, royal lilies, sea holly, lupines, Oriental poppies, foxglove, thalictrum, and yellow meadow rue. At the end of the path is an arbor and reflecting pool, adorned by a statue of a bathing maiden known as "Barefoot Kate."

Below the cherry walk on the lowest level is a sizable rose garden, constructed in 1910 and focusing on a fountain pool and a loggia where weekend guests of the Vanderbilts, after completing a tour of the gardens, could relax over a cup of tea. The beds are devoted to an array of hybrid roses, among them red 'Love' and 'Milestone', pink 'Promise', pinkish-orange 'Fascination' and yellow 'Oregold'.

In 1984 the Frederick W. Vanderbilt Garden Association, a group of volunteers, began a project to restore the gardens to their former glory (no small task, considering that of the estate's 60 employees in Vanderbilt's day more than half worked on the grounds). The annual beds were replanted in 1985; the cherry tree walk and pool garden were restored the following year with 4,000 perennial plants; the rose garden was completed in 1987 with more than 1,000 bushes, many labeled with their donors' names.

Vanderbilt would have been pleased. A man who cared little for the glittering social whirl of his wealthy peers, he preferred quiet walks around his private domain, often sharing thoughts with his gardeners about the flowers and vegetables they raised. They must have been good ones. Year after year, Vanderbilt entries carried off honors at the Dutchess County Horticultural Society's annual flower show and the Dutchess County Fair.

❖ VANDERBILT MANSION NATIONAL HISTORIC SITE, Rte. 9. Administered by the National Park Service, 519 Albany Post Rd., Hyde Park, NY 12538. Tel. (914) 229-9115. **Facilities**: Gift shop, picnic area near the river's edge, rest rooms. Generally accessible to the handicapped. **Open**: Grounds are open daily year-round, 9 a.m. to dusk. Admission free. A fee is charged for tours of the mansion, which is open 9 a.m. to 5 p.m. Wednesday through Sunday year-round. Closed New Year's Day, Thanksgiving, and Christmas. **Directions**: From Poughkeepsie (junction of routes 9 and 44/55) go 7 miles north on Rte. 9, 2 miles beyond FDR home, and look for sign on left. By train, take the Hudson line to Poughkeepsie and a taxi (5 miles) from there. Metro-North Railroad runs Saturday tours of the Roosevelt Homes and Vanderbilt Mansion from May 20 to October 28.

VANDERBILT MANSION, HYDE PARK

INNISFREE, MILLBROOK

Hidden away up a country lane near Millbrook, New York, is one of the most startlingly beautiful of the Hudson Valley's gardens: a 200-acre landscape centered on a hill-girdled lake—a place where visitors make their own discoveries as they stroll from one carefully planned "picture" to the next.

Innisfree, named for Yeats's Irish "isle of peace," was the inspiration of Walter Beck, a professional artist whose father had been a landscape gardener in Ohio. In 1922, at the age of 58, Beck had the good fortune to marry Marion Burt Stone, a wealthy divorcée who owned the lake and a thousand acres around it. Deciding to make Innisfree their home (except for winters on Park Avenue) the Becks began building a Queen Anne mansion with formal gardens. While the work went on, they lived in an older cottage nearby.

Gradually, however, Walter began to feel that something was missing, that English formality was not quite suited to Innisfree's spectacular natural surroundings—and to his own developing sense of art, which had been increasingly influenced by the spontaneous brushstrokes of the Orient. On a trip to London Beck happened across some scroll paintings of an eighth-century garden created by a poet-painter named Wang Wei. He was immediately struck by the ancient Chinese concept of a "cup garden," in which smaller, self-contained landscapes make three-dimensional pictures within a larger, harmonious frame.

Thus inspired, Beck set about transforming Innisfree. Marion took an enthusiastic part, suggesting specific plantings and colors to carry out each scheme. By 1929 Beck had some 30 men working on his projects, building a 7-acre holding pond in the hills behind the mansion to feed a network of streams and waterfalls. He and his workmen combed the forests and fields for rocks that were moved by tractor and jacked into

Rustic chairs of a timeless design are placed everywhere on the trail. Opposite above: An Oriental sculpture adorns a rock at Innisfree, set off by clematis blooms. Below: Plant specimens chosen for their shapes, colors, and textures adorn the foundations of the Innisfree mansion, which was torn down when it proved hard to maintain.

place as sculptural elements—then adjusted under the owner's direction so their distinctive shapes would come alive. On a small point jutting into the lake, he installed a grouping of irregular boulders he called Owl, Turtle, and Dragon Rocks, posing them in asymetrical tension so as "to hold in balance the lake and the nearby hills."

Walter Beck died in 1954. His wife, determined to share Innisfree with the public, set up a foundation under the direction of Lester Collins, a former chairman of Harvard's Department of Landscape Architecture and a longtime friend. To keep the foundation going through difficult times, 750 acres of woodlands were sold to Rockefeller University for use as a field research station in 1972; a decade later the old Queen Anne mansion, which had proved both esthetically discon-certing and expensive to maintain, was torn down. Collins, however, was able to preserve Beck's finest landscape features, and to add others in the same spirit, including a new stream, three waterfalls, and a tall jet foun-tain on a wooded island across the lake, which, in the absence of the mansion, is now dramatically established as the center of the scheme.

From a grassy parking area where they can pick up self-guiding maps, visitors cross to a picnic site that commands a fine view of the lake, then descend a path to the right through a rustic wisteria arch. Clustered around the north side of the lake are a wealth of pictures: a "mist fountain" spuming from a high outcrop; a steep rock garden with a waterfall; a sinuous stream curving through irises and primroses; and a whole series of gardens built on the terraced foundations of the old mansion, set off by a lotus pool. On the promontory below are a mysterious "mountain" built of open stonework as well as Beck's favorite Owl, Turtle, and Dragon Rocks.

Strollers can continue around the lake, crossing a bridge to the soft, scented shade of Pine Island, crossing back by a whimsical covered bridge built in the shape of a corncrib, and returning to the parking lot through a dark hemlock grove. Everywhere along the trail, rustic chairs and benches are placed to encourage visitors to pause and savor the views—of trees, rocks, and wild flowers, sun on wind-riffled water, clouds in a summer sky. And that, in the end, is what Innisfree is about.

❖ INNISFREE, Tyrrel Rd., Millbrook, NY 12545. Tel. (914) 677-8000. **Facilities**: Lovely picnic area overlooking lake; rustic chairs and benches at many vantage points. Portable toilets near parking lot. Limited access to the handicapped on paths. **Open**: May 1 through October 20, Wednesday through Friday, 10 a.m. to 4 p.m., Saturday and Sunday, 11 a.m. to 5 p.m. Admission charged. Closed Monday and Tuesday except legal holidays. **Directions**: From Taconic State Parkway, take Millbrook exit, east 1¼ miles on Rte. 44, right on Tyrell Road, 1 mile to entrance. From the east, Tyrell Road is on the left, 2½ miles from South Millbrook on Rte. 44.

INNISFREE, MILLBROOK

❖

MARY FLAGLER CARY ARBORETUM, MILLBROOK

The Perennial Garden at the Cary Arboretum is a collection of some 1,000 species and varieties, illustrating the relationship between plant adaptation and horticultural design.
Below: Varieties of iris form a border backed by lilacs.

On her death in 1967, Mary Flagler Cary, an heiress of Standard Oil and Florida real estate, left her summer retreat of 2,000 acres in Millbrook to be preserved for the public weal. The New York Botanical Garden was assigned to administer the land, and thus the Mary Flagler Cary Arboretum was born.

A trip to the arboretum, site of the internationally renowned Institute of Ecosystem Studies (IES), is a pleasant day's outing. The visit starts at Gifford House, an attractive early-nineteenth-century brick home remodeled into an information and education center. Here visitors obtain free passes and maps, browse through gift and plant shops, and stroll through the extensive Perennial Garden, whose display of some 1,000 species and cultivars is one of the largest and most instructive in the Northeast.

Ranging around and behind the parking lot is the Howard Taylor Lilac Collection, consisting of 60 different French hybrids as well as important species and early crosses, which perfume the air from mid-May to early June. In the shade along the entrance walk are many types of hostas valued for their decorative foliage, including the yellowish green 'Sum and Substance', the bluish green 'Blue Mammoth', the yellowish 'Sun Power' and the yellow-edged 'Resonance'.

Directly back of the house is a fine array of peonies, among them tree peonies and single, double, semidouble, Japanese, and anemone types, as well as a demonstration garden of low-maintenance perennials that thrive under a wide range of conditions with little care. Near these are a mixed border and a long pergola that displays varieties of clematis and other important vines.

A large area of the garden is devoted to shade-loving perennials, including a rhododendron collection planted by the Garden Clubs of Orange and Dutchess counties, along with other species like bergenias, athyriums, brunneras, dicentras, epimediums, astilbes, dwarf iris, and phlox. Ranged about the perimeter are a formal herb garden with culinary, medicinal, cosmetic, and decorative herbs, and an area showing hybrid day lilies in varying colors and forms. The Shankman Rose Garden, an ecological demonstration bed for testing organic vs. chemical treatment of roses, features modern hybrid teas, grandifloras, and floribundas.

Around the center of the garden, one bed shows off ornamental grasses that are hardy in the region; another displays a wide range of perenni-

MARY FLAGLER CARY ARBORETUM,
MILLBROOK

als that thrive in sun. In still other beds are species that attract hummingbirds, including monarda, heuchera, columbine, penstemon, and cardinal flower, and varieties favored by butterflies, among them dianthus, sedums, yarrows, and primulas.

At the back of the Perennial Garden is a demonstration of common woody ornamentals for evaluating their resistance to browsing by deer. The field beyond is used for the Institute's Outdoor Science Center, where a series of "mini ponds" demonstrates the effects of nutrients on aquatic ecosystems. The center has proved a popular part of the Institute's education program, which also offers a wide range of classes and activities for both children and adults.

From Gifford House you can set out, on foot or by car, to explore other areas of the arboretum, whose rolling woods and meadows are threaded by the scenic East Branch of Wappinger Creek. An especially popular spot is the Fern Glen, where plants indigenous to the northeastern United States are grown in their natural habitats. Highlights include a pond, limestone and acid cobbles, wild flower beds, a shrub swamp, and a bog, all surrounded by a hemlock forest. Stop for a moment in the coolness of the hemlock grove, where a rustic deck with Adirondack chairs overlooks the rushing waters of the creek.

To complete a tour of the Institute's public areas, take the main interior road, along which are planted collections of different birches and pines and a fine array of willows—the latter boasting 17 species from North America, 34 from Eurasia, 7 from Japan and Korea, and 35 horticultural crosses and cultivars. The final stop, just across Route 82, is the IES greenhouse, where you can see colorful tropical plants, others being raised for outdoor displays, and still others for use in controlled ecological research.

❖ INSTITUTE OF ECOSYSTEM STUDIES, Mary Flagler Cary Arboretum, Rte. 44A, Box R, Millbrook, NY 12545-0178. Tel. (914) 677-5359. **Facilities**: Plant shop, gift shop, picnic area, rest rooms. Ecology education programs for adults and children. The IES Plant Science Building offers periodic exhibits. **Open**: May through September, Monday through Saturday, 9 a.m. to 6 p.m.; Sunday, 1 p.m.

to 6 p.m. October through April, Monday through Saturday, 9 a.m. to 4 p.m.; Sunday 1 p.m. to 4 p.m. Closed on public holidays. Admission free. Free permits available until one hour before closing. **Directions**: From the Taconic State Parkway, take the Millbrook exit, go east on Rte. 44, north (left) on Rte. 44A. Gifford House is the next driveway past the IES Plant Science Building on the left. From Rte. 22 at Amenia, go west on Rte. 44 and straight onto Rte. 44A, which bypasses the village of Millbrook.

Below: Small knot gardens of begonias and boxwood adorn the Inner Garden adjoining the house at Wethersfield.

❖

WETHERSFIELD, AMENIA

One of the latest gardens in the region to be opened to the public is at Wethersfield, the 1,200-acre country residence of the late Chauncey D. Stillman. Modeled after villa gardens of the Italian Renaissance, it is built not around splashy displays of flowers but around trimmed specimens and hedges in different shades of green, accented by sculptures, pavilions, fountains, and carefully framed views of rolling farmlands and woods.

Adjoining the mansion is an intimate Inner Garden, designed by Brian Lynch at the same time the house was built in 1939–40. The lawn is laid out in a keyhole shape edged by perennial beds. On one side is a small reflecting pool with a redstone statue nicknamed the "Pink Lady"; on the other is a tunnel-like arbor of European beech. An upper level provides space for more statuary and four small knot garden beds.

The main attraction at Wethersfield, however, are the formal Italian gardens designed by Evelyn Poehler and developed over a quarter century beginning in 1947. Laid out on a long axis to the east of the house, they form a series of outdoor rooms that visitors can stroll through at their leisure, pausing to admire new vistas on every side. A major focal point is

An elliptical water garden is a major focal point of the overall design. Beyond the steps are flowering dogwoods and Wethersfield's most striking feature: a long allée of arborvitae, clipped into walls of greenery 23 feet tall.

an elliptical water garden near the center, which opens to the south over sweeping lawns to a panorama of fields and hills.

To the north of the water garden, heralded by a flight of broad steps and a pair of ornate cupid urns, is the garden's most striking feature: a long, grassy allée of arborvitae, clipped into solid walls of greenery 23 feet high, that leads to another elliptical space at the end. Here, in a raised pool with softly jetting fountains, is a naiad by the distinguished Swedish sculptor Carl Milles.

While wandering through the gardens, keep an eye out for two pairs of free-ranging peacocks—one pair a standard blue, the other white—that Mr. Stillman liked to have around. And don't fail to stroll around the perimeter and into the fields below the house, where the Stillmans took their daily horseback or carriage rides to savor the views. Here is a wild woodland area marked by Tuscan columns and still more sculptures along its trails.

❖ WETHERSFIELD, Pugsley Hill Rd., Amenia, NY 12501. Tel. (914) 373-8037. **Facilities**: Picnic grove, rest rooms. Accessible to the handicapped. **Open**: Wednesday, Friday, and Saturday, noon to 5 p.m., June through September. Group tours by reservation. Admission charged. **Directions**: From Millbrook (Taconic State Parkway exit), drive east on Rte. 44 for 6 miles, left on Rte. 86 to Pugsley Hill Rd. and follow signs. From Amenia (Rte. 22), go west on Rte. 44 for 3 miles, right on Rte. 86 to Pugsley Hill Rd.

❖

MONTGOMERY PLACE, ANNANDALE-ON-HUDSON

"Of all the fine estates along this portion of the Hudson, this is said to be the most perfect in its beauty and arrangements. Waterfalls, picturesque bridges, romantic glens, groves, a magnificent park, one of the most beautiful of the ornamental gardens in this country, and views of the river and the mountains, unsurpassed, render Montgomery Place a retreat to be coveted, even by the most favoured of fortune."

So wrote historian Benson Lossing in his 1866 treatise *The Hudson From the Wilderness to the Sea*. Landscaper Andrew Jackson Downing declared the estate "nowhere surpassed in America in point of location, natural beauty, or landscape gardening charms." With the addition of fine gardens in the 1920s and 1930s, painstakingly restored by Historic Hudson Valley, Inc. and opened to the public in 1988, this 434-acre showpiece is probably the most richly varied, and closest to perfection, of any of the river's great country seats.

It all started when Janet Livingston Montgomery—widow of Revolutionary War hero General Richard Montgomery—purchased a farm north of Rhinebeck in 1802. Raised at Clermont, the Livingston manor a few miles farther north (see section on Clermont), she adorned

MID-HUDSON EAST

the property with an elegant new mansion in the Federal style. She also brought a family love of horticulture to her new home, adding to the farm's thriving orchards her own commercial nursery, which for years supplied seeds, bulbs, and fruit trees to other homeowners eager to improve their grounds.

On Janet's death her brother Edward Livingston, U.S. Secretary of State and Minister to France, took over the property and enthusiastically set about turning it into a "pleasure ground." When Edward died unexpectedly the next year, his wife, Louise, daughter Coralie and son-in-law Thomas Barton carried on, calling on their friend Downing for landscaping advice as well as nursery plants. Downing marveled at the miles of scenic trails that had been cut through the woods to reveal views of a cascading stream, two pretty ponds, and the Hudson River below.

The Delafields, descendants of the Livingstons, continued to improve Montgomery Place. Most of the present gardens were the inspiration of Violetta White Delafield, a talented gardener and amateur botanist, who inherited the estate in 1921. She turned her attention to an overgrown swale beside the mile-long approach to the house, which presents a parklike aspect with magnificent black locusts, sycamores, oaks, and other specimen trees. Here she transformed an eyesore into a pretty woodland garden laced with paths, stone steps, and a man-made brook, planting it with trilliums, primulas, Canada lilies, ferns, hostas, rhododendrons, and early spring bulbs. She named her creation the Rough Garden when she discovered how quickly it could be overrun by weeds.

At the south end of the Rough Garden, the main path ascends stepping stones to emerge in an area Violetta named the Ellipse, a quiet oval of lawn framed by dark hemlocks and centering on an oval pool graced by water lilies, irises, and day lilies, with a single flowering dogwood at its edge.

From the Ellipse a path continues through a grape arbor to Violetta's formal gardens, which she began in 1929. Directly ahead is her wisteria-covered potting shed and greenhouse, which has been restored and now supplies plants for Montgomery Place as well as other showpieces maintained by Historic Hudson Valley. To the left is the Rose Garden, in whose symmetrical beds she arranged old-fashioned varieties by color—

Wicker chairs under a portico of the house at Montgomery Place provide a pleasant spot from which to savor the river view.

MONTGOMERY PLACE,
ANNANDALE-ON-HUDSON

A decorative perennial border.

red, pink, yellow, and white—bordering them with a hedge of Marquise de Bocella, an 1842 pink hybrid perpetual the family adopted and christened the "Livingston Rose."

To the right is the Herb Garden, which Violetta created in 1939. It has been carefully reconstructed according to the plan she drew, with some 40 varieties of herbs around a central sundial. Faithfully reproduced are the original brick paths, which Violetta had instructed her mason to lay in a slightly undulating pattern to soften the garden's straight lines. Beside and beyond this garden is a series of decorative perennial borders, including displays of pillar roses, delphiniums, peonies, and irises, all dominated by a large tulip tree more than a century and a half old. Tucked away in a far corner are four small headstones that memorialize four family favorites of Montgomery Place, three dogs and a cat.

For those who would like to explore the site's abundant natural beauties, there are free maps in boxes at the head of the walking trails. Notable are the spectacular cataracts of the Saw Kill River on the northern edge of the property, the open western meadows and the South Woods, more than 80 acres of unspoiled native forest with trees several centuries old.

❖ MONTGOMERY PLACE, River Road, P.O. Box 32, Annandale-on-Hudson, NY 12504. Tel. (914) 758-5461. Administered by Historic Hudson Valley, 150 White Plains Rd., Tarrytown, NY 10591. Tel. (914) 631-8200. **Facilities:** Visitor center with a gift shop and rest rooms, a shady picnic grove with tables nearby. Guided tours of grounds and mansion. Old-fashioned games like croquet, badminton, French hoops, and Chinese checkers are provided free for guests to play. Sunday afternoon garden workshops. The grounds and formal gardens are generally accessible to the handicapped (the woodland trails are difficult). In the fall visitors can pick their own apples in Montgomery Place's extensive orchards, or buy apples, pears, peaches, and other seasonal produce at a wayside stand. **Open:** Daily except Tuesday, April through October, 10 a.m. to 5 p.m. (until sunset on summer weekends). Open weekends only during November and December. Closed January through March. Admission charged. **Directions:** Off Rte. 9G 3 miles north of Kingston-Rhinecliff Bridge. From the New York State Thruway, take Exit 19 to Rte. 209 North/199 to the bridge; continue on Rte. 199 across bridge for 2 miles, turn left on Rte. 9G and go 3 miles, then left on Annandale Rd. and bear left to entrance. From the Taconic State Parkway, take Red Hook/Pine Plains Exit to Rte. 199, go west 10 miles through Red Hook to Rte. 9G, turn right on 9G 1 mile to Annandale Rd., turn left and bear left to entrance. By train from Penn Station, take Amtrak to Rhinecliff station and a taxi from there.

MONTGOMERY PLACE,
ANNANDALE-ON-HUDSON

❖

CLERMONT, GERMANTOWN

*Opposite: In Clermont's
Long View, tall locusts frame
a striking glimpse of the river
and a lone mountain peak on
the opposite shore. Tables and
benches are arranged for
picnickers to enjoy the view.
Below: A blaze of day lilies.*

The section of the river from Hyde Park to Hudson is sometimes referred to as "Livingston Valley"—at one time members of that family occupied no less than 40 mansions along its eastern bank. While most of the houses are gone or in other hands today, the oldest, Clermont, the home of seven generations of Livingstons, is now maintained as a public historic site.

In 1686 Robert Livingston, an enterprising Scottish trader, managed to acquire a royal patent to 160,000 acres that stretched from the Hudson to the Massachusetts/Connecticut line. Over the years Clermont, a portion of his private empire, passed down to his great grandson Robert R. Livingston, Jr., one of the drafters of the Declaration of Independence. Robert R. was the family's most distinguished member, serving as Chancellor of New York, U.S. Secretary of Foreign Affairs, and Minister to France. He also backed a young inventor named Robert Fulton in building the first successful steamboat, a development that was to alter the quiet life of the Hudson as nothing had before. On its maiden voyage from New York to Albany in 1807 it made a special stop at the dock below the Chancellor's house. Fulton later christened the boat the *Clermont* in his honor.

The estate remained in the hands of Livingston descendants until 1962, when it was acquired by the state and carefully restored. Aside from the old mansion, the finest aspect of the property is its unusual view to the south—down a long, bowl-like meadow once grazed by sheep, where tall locusts frame an exquisite view of the river and a solitary mountain peak on the opposite shore. Above the Long View, as it is called, ample picnic areas overlook the Lilac Walk, where an impressive collection of old species puts on a fragrant show each May, as well as broad, grassy slopes that are blanketed with day lilies later on. Below the

meadow, where the land drops off again, a gravel path leads down to the river near the site of the Chancellor's dock.

On a trip to Clermont, don't fail to stop at the carriage barn, nicely refurbished as a visitor center, where exhibits, family photographs, and a short film starring present-day Livingstons recall the good old days. From here one can stroll to the house, which is set off by many fine specimen trees, among them an ancient black walnut of massive size, and, on the bank above, several umbrella magnolias that bear large white flowers and pink pineapple-like fruits.

North of the house lies a series of gardens developed in the 1930s by Clermont's last owner, Alice Delafield Clarkson Livingston, and restored with the help of her daughter, Honoria Livingston McVitty. These include a walled perennial garden in the English tradition, a wooded "wilderness" garden with wild flowers and bulbs, and an upper cutting garden of peonies, roses, irises, zinnias, and other varieties used in flower arrangements for the house. Above the garden are the picturesque remains of an old greenhouse, and a small playhouse where Honoria remembers spending many happy hours as a child.

CLERMONT, GERMANTOWN

❖ CLERMONT STATE HISTORIC SITE, 1 Clermont Ave., Germantown, NY 12526. Tel. (518) 537-4240. **Facilities**: Visitor center with historical exhibits and a gift shop. Scenic picnic areas with tables, cooking grills, rest rooms. Miles of walking trails. The main grounds are generally accessible to the handicapped. **Open**: Grounds open all year, 8:30 a.m. to sunset. Admission free. Mansion and visitor center open for touring mid-April through Labor Day, Wednesday through Saturday 10 a.m. to 5 p.m., Sunday, noon to 5 p.m. From Labor Day through the end of October, Wednesday to Sunday noon to 5 p.m. Many special interpretive events scheduled throughout the season. **Directions**: Located off County Rte. 6, just west of Rte. 9G, midway between the Rip Van Winkle and Kingston-Rhinecliff bridges. Take New York State Thruway Exit 19 or 21, or exit the Taconic State Parkway at Rte. 199 (Red Hook).

OLANA, HUDSON

"About an hour this side of Albany is the center of the world—I own it."

Like a fairy castle, Olana rises on a hilltop, set off by a slope carpeted in golden yellow coreopsis.

When Frederic Edwin Church penned those words to a friend in 1869, they were only partly in jest. The most famous artist of the Hudson River School, Church had made a fortune from his heroic paintings of natural wonders like the Andes and Niagara Falls. He invested much of it in a hillside farm across the Hudson from the village of Catskill, a 250-acre property that encapsulated the river's majesties and provided a retreat where he and his family could spend the rest of their lives.

At the top of the hill, 500 feet above the river, Church and architect Calvert Vaux built a fantastic castle in Persian style, which his wife, Isabel, christened "Olana" after an ancient Middle Eastern fortress and treasure house. From his studio Church could paint the valley in all its changing moods, from blazing mountain sunsets to sudden, swirling storms.

Over nearly four decades, until his death in 1900, Church came to regard Olana as his masterpiece—a living composition in three dimensions in the "picturesque" style, an idealized, natural-appearing design approach popularized by Andrew Jackson Downing and dear to the hearts of American Romanticists. Even when frail health and arthritis cut down on his painting, he was still busy building more than seven miles of carriage drives, planting trees, and arranging surprise vistas for his guests, declaring that he could make "more and better landscapes in this way than by tampering with paint and canvas in the studio."

Both Church and his wife were enchanted by nature's feast of colors, and Isabel was fond of growing her own flowers, too. Behind the house, over a stone retaining wall, her love is preserved in a semicircular "min-

gled" or "scatter" garden she started in the 1880s, which is planted with old roses, peonies, cosmos, bee balm, torenias, nasturtiums, dahlias, cleomes, phlox, sweet alyssum, and marigolds.

Below the house and garden, the sloping, parklike meadows are blanketed in wild flowers from spring through fall—red clover, yellow coreopsis, daisies, Queen Anne's lace, purple asters, goldenrod. Here and there are domesticated plantings from earlier days: forsythia, lilac, bottlebrush, trumpet vine, and an orchard of flowering apple trees. At the foot of the hill is a picturesque lake, created out of a swampy area for family boating, picnics, and skating as well as a source of water and ice for the farm. Like most of Church's landscaping efforts, it was also a calculated artistic touch: besides reflecting light and passing clouds as a focal point in itself, its contours closely mirror the lakelike widening of the Hudson called Bend in the River, drawing the eye out to the grand climax of Olana's view.

Opposite: Olana's splendid isolation is reflected in this aerial view, with the Hudson River in the background. Above: From his studio, Church could paint the valley in all its changing moods, including the light that comes before a storm.

❖ **OLANA STATE HISTORIC SITE**, R.D. 2, Hudson, NY 12534. Tel. (518) 828-0135. **Facilities**: Gift shop, rest rooms. Limited access to the handicapped. **Open**: Grounds open daily 8 a.m. to sunset. Admission free. Mansion open mid-April through October, except Mondays and Tuesdays; Wednesday through Saturday 10 a.m. to 5 p.m.; Sunday noon to 5 p.m.; noon to 5 p.m. Wednesday through Sunday after Labor Day weekend to October 31. Admission charged. **Directions**: From the Taconic State Parkway, take Hudson exit to Rte. 23, west to Rte. 9G south. From the New York State Thruway, take Exit 21, cross the Rip Van Winkle Bridge to Rte. 9G south. By train from Penn Station, take Amtrak to the Hudson station and a taxi (5 miles) from there.

OLANA, HUDSON

❖

S K Y L A N D S   B O T A N I C A L
G A R D E N ,   R I N G W O O D ,   N.J.

*Opposite: A quiet spot at
Skylands is enhanced by a
low wall, a statue, and the
sight of autumn leaves falling
from gracefully weeping trees.
Below: To the south, a series
of formal gardens steps down
from the mansion. Above the
balustrade is an allée of
towering magnolias; below is
a pool for water lilies.*

While most of the showplace estates open to the public are
on the eastern shore of the Hudson, a notable exception
is Skylands, a horticultural extravaganza tucked away in
the rolling Ramapo Mountains where northern New
Jersey meets New York. The feudal domain of two successive millionaires
with more than a casual eye for floral beauty—both were trustees and
supporters of The New York Botanical Garden—it was deemed worthy
enough to be designated New Jersey's own Botanical Garden in 1984,
with 5,000 species and varieties adorning a host of formal gardens as
well as wilder meadows and woods.

Skylands' first owner was Francis Lynde Stetson, J. P. Morgan's
lawyer, who in 1891 began assembling several farmsteads into a thou-
sand-acre estate. Stetson's original notion was to make it into a private
enclave for summer homes like Tuxedo Park, which had been started several years earlier a few miles to the north, but he soon decided to keep
the land for himself. He built a 34-room Victorian mansion and hired
Samuel Parsons, Jr., a protégé of Frederick Law Olmsted, to lay out the
grounds, which included a nine-hole private golf course (kept in trim by
Mrs. Stetson's flock of Shropshire sheep), a formal rose garden, 28
miles of scenic carriage roads, plantings of 20,000 evergreens, extensive
orchards, and a large working farm. A Stetson friend, steel magnate
Andrew Carnegie, pronounced it "the most beautiful country estate in
America."

In 1922 Skylands was acquired by Clarence McKenzie Lewis, a New

York investment banker, who replaced Stetson's house with an even larger Tudor mansion and hired the prominent firm of Vitale and Geiffert to
design new gardens about the grounds. An avid horticulturist—he kept
60 gardeners busy—Lewis spent the next three decades collecting prized
plants from locales as varied as the New Jersey Barrens and Afghanistan,
trying anything he liked if he thought it had the least chance of surviving
in the Ramapos. Evidence of his plantsmanship are three varieties unique
to the estate: a climbing hydrangea, *Hydrangea petiolaris* 'Skylands
Giant', which grows on the west side of the manor near the flagpole; a
golden form of Oriental spruce, *Picea orientalis* 'Skylands', in the vicinity
of the pump house and the volunteer greenhouse; and a dark purple
dwarf iris, *Iris cristata* 'Skylands Iris', which can be found in the
Octagonal Garden.

A stroll around the property reveals these treasures and many more.
North of the mansion is the Winter Garden, where 30 varieties of trees
and shrubs notable for form, texture, and foliage color—ranging from

SKYLANDS   BOTANICAL   GARDEN,
RINGWOOD, N.J.

blue to gold to red to every shade of green—provided Lewis with a lively vista from his library window during the colder months.

To the south a series of formal gardens steps down the slope from the house. In the Octagonal Garden a sculpture fountain is surrounded by waist-high stone beds that show off a fine collection of dwarf shrubs and small rock-garden plants. Along Magnolia Walk, almost 300 feet long, sweet bay magnolias rise above beds of hostas, their creamy white blossoms perfuming the air in June. Below stretches the Azalea Garden, ablaze in May with azaleas and rhododendrons banked along a water lily pool. Completing the sequence is a Summer Garden with multihued day lilies in clipped yew parterres, and a Peony Garden lined by shrubby Chinese tree peonies leading to a 25-foot semicircular stone bench, backed by hemlocks that terminate the view.

From here one emerges, through a lilac collection of 60 varieties, to the estate's main interior road, which is bordered by an imposing array of flowering shrubs. Across the road are the Perennial Borders and a large Annual Garden, planted in different color schemes each year around an antique Roman wellhead, which forms an axis with a statue of Diana to the east. Behind these gardens is the spectacular Crab Apple Vista, refurbished in 1987 with a double line of trees, 166 in all, which form an avenue of pink blossoms a half mile long in early May.

Still farther to the east visitors can explore the Rhododendron and Heather Gardens, continuing on trails through a woodland Wildflower Garden centered on a bog and pond that are surrounded by trilliums, primroses, and ferns. Before returning to the parking lot, true plant lovers may want to wander through the lower meadows, where they will find willows and horse chestnuts—and, if they're lucky, rare fringed gentians poking up in the field.

❖ SKYLANDS BOTANICAL GARDEN, Ringwood State Park, Box 1304, Ringwood, NJ 07456. Tel. (201) 962-7031. For garden information, call (201) 962-7527 or 962-9534. **Facilities**: Visitor center with exhibits, gift shop, and rest rooms; open on Sunday afternoons, 1 p.m. to 4 p.m. Guided tours of the gardens on Sundays at 2 p.m. Accessible to the handicapped except for some garden steps and trails.

Open: Daily, 8 a.m. to 8 p.m. Admission free, except on designated weekends, Memorial Day to Labor Day. **Directions**: From the New York State Thruway, take Exit 15A (Suffern), go north on Rte. 17 to Sloatsburg, take Ringwood exit west on Rte. 72 to Skylands sign. From the George Washington Bridge, take Rtes. 4 and 208 north to 287 South to Exit 57 (Skyline Drive) to end, right around reservoir, right on Sloatsburg Rd. to Skylands sign.

❖

STORM KING ART CENTER, MOUNTAINVILLE

F our hundred acres of fields and woodlands, embraced by rolling hills, form a dramatic backdrop for Storm King's collection of contemporary sculpture, which consists of more than a hundred outdoor pieces done by leading artists from 1945 on. The works, many of heroic scale, are given plenty of elbow room, and they seem to take on added intensity from their natural surroundings of space, sunlight, and clouds. Together, they draw visitors of all ages, challenging people to use their imagination and have a little fun.

The idea for Storm King was conceived by the late Ralph Ogden, an art collector, and Peter Stern, his partner in Star Expansion Company, a manufacturer of metal fasteners in Mountainville, New York. The art works are exhibited in open-air "galleries" developed with the help of landscape architect William A. Rutherford over the last three decades. Entering the park, visitors are welcomed by *The Arch*, a monumental, 56-foot-high piece that was the last stabile completed by Alexander Calder before his death in 1976. An untitled piece by Robert Grosvenor, black, brooding, and bridge-like, spans a field on the right; in the far dis-

Henry Moore's Reclining Connected Forms, 1969, *is set off by trees and clumps of flowering rhododendron.*

Various striking modern sculptures dot the rolling meadows at Storm King Art Center.

tance rise Mark di Suvero's girder constructions *Mon Pere, Mon Pere* and *Mother Peace*. Farther up the road, the shiny red cylinders of *Iliad* by Alexander Liberman stand out vividly against green lawns.

On the north hillside is Alice Aycock's exuberant *Threefold Manifestation II*. At the top of a central hill is the museum building, a Norman-style residence built in 1935 by a New York lawyer named Vermont Hatch, whose estate was purchased in 1960 by the Ralph E. Ogden Foundation and given to Storm King. The center takes its name from Storm King Mountain, the famous landmark that lies on the river two miles east.

The lawn around and behind the mansion is a landscape of flowering rhododendrons, dogwoods, and tall specimen trees. In addition to five more pieces by Calder, this area highlights the work of David Smith, who pioneered new approaches in abstract metal sculpture from 1954 to 1965. Here, too, are works by other major artists, including *City on the High Mountain* by Louise Nevelson and *Reclining Connected Forms* by Henry Moore.

Nearby is Isamu Noguchi's *Momo Taro*, a 40-ton composition of granite that was specially commissioned for Storm King; it has become a particular favorite of children, who are invited to feel it, clamber over it, and climb inside. From its mounded vantage point one can look down on Kenneth Snelson's *Free Ride Home*, and across a long, grassy vista to another bright red Liberman titled *Adam*, which is framed against the dark treeline on a rise. North of this area, works by a score of other artists are sited along gravel walking paths.

For those interested in exploring further, the Mountainville Conservancy of Storm King Art Center has preserved 2,300 acres of Schunnemunk Mountain two miles to the west. Intended as a haven for the study and enjoyment of native flora and fauna, it has 20 miles of trails. Trail maps are sold in the Art Center's museum shop.

❖ STORM KING ART CENTER, Old Pleasant Hill Rd., Mountainville, NY 10953. Tel. (914) 534-3190. **Facilities**: Museum shop, indoor sculpture galleries, picnic areas, rest rooms. Limited access to the handicapped. For a free calendar of events—which include guided tours, lectures, concerts, videos, and horticulture talks—call the number above. **Open**: Daily from 11 a.m. to 5:30 p.m., April 1 to November 15; until 8 p.m. on Saturdays in June, July, and August. Closed November 16 to March 31. Admission charged. **Directions**: From the south, take New York State Thruway to Exit 16, north on Rte. 32 for 10 miles, and follow Storm King Art Center signs. From the north, New York State Thruway to Exit 17, east on Rte. 17K to center of Newburgh, south on Rte. 32 for 5 miles and follow signs. From upper Westchester and Connecticut, west on I-84 across Newburgh-Beacon Bridge, Exit 10S south on Rte. 32 for 7 miles and follow signs. By bus from Port Authority Bus Terminal, take the ShortLine bus which stops at Storm King.

STORM KING ART CENTER,
MOUNTAINVILLE

❖

MOHONK MOUNTAIN HOUSE, NEW PALTZ

"I have treated this property, the result of 76 purchases, as a landscape artist does his canvas, only my canvas covers seven square miles."

Much of the charm of Mohonk Mountain House is embodied in its ornate Victorian gardens.

So wrote Albert K. Smiley, who with his twin brother, Alfred, discovered a small inn on a spectacular lake in the Shawangunk Mountains in 1869. Falling in love with the scenery as a spot for a summer home, they bought the inn and 300 acres for $28,000. The two Quaker schoolteachers soon found themselves in the resort business for which they had neither experience nor taste. Observed Albert, "I had no more thought of it than going to the moon."

Nevertheless, in the 12 decades that followed, the Smileys and their descendants—all staunch believers in God and Nature—carefully developed and nurtured their land. Today it has grown to 2,200 acres, surrounded by 25,000 acres of wilderness, offering 85 miles of hiking trails and other wholesome activities that range from tennis and croquet to carriage rides and paddle-boating on the lake. The modest inn has become a rambling Victorian castle accommodating 500 overnight guests, who eat in a large family dining hall and relax on verandas in rocking chairs to view the lake to the east and highland sunsets to the west. Mohonk Mountain House is proud of its designation as a National Historic Landmark. And indeed there is nothing quite like it anywhere.

It was in Mohonk's gardens, begun in 1883, that Albert and his half brother, Daniel, took their greatest pride ("Gardening, with Mr. Smiley, was dangerously near a passion," wrote a family biographer in 1911). The rocky land was so inhospitable that at first all they could manage was a small bed of geraniums, which Albert liked to grumble cost him

MOHONK MOUNTAIN HOUSE,
NEW PALTZ

Among the Victorian favorites planted at Mohonk are tall foxgloves (Digitalis purpurea), *which come in shades of maroon, pink, and white.*

"about $5 per bloom." Undaunted, they hauled in hundreds of wagon loads of topsoil from elsewhere on the property and gradually coaxed into life 25 acres of gardens and lawns.

On his frequent walks Albert carried a pair of pruning shears, always ready to discipline an errant shrub or harvest a particularly beautiful rose. The whole Smiley family came to indulge "A.K." in his passion. It was a standing joke that whenever some hotel expense had to be justified, he would reply: "Thee may charge it to the flower garden." Though other departments were held strictly accountable, the rewards of flowers were not measured in dollars but, as he put it, in "a long life and abounding health."

The gardens today remain true to A.K.'s plans, offering a living portrait of the landscapes of yesteryear. (Before setting out to explore the grounds, stop at the greenhouse gift shop and pick up one or more of Ruth Smiley's charming self-guiding booklets, which include "The Mohonk Gardens" and the "Fern/Wildflower Trail.")

The centerpiece is a large Show Garden, which a grounds crew keeps ablaze with color from late May through fall, reaching a peak at the height of the tourist season in August. Some 75 beds feature a variety of annuals and biennials, all neatly labeled, that reflect Victorian tastes— dazzling orange, yellow, and scarlet celosias, purplish nierembergias, dark blue and burgundy salvias, vivid yellow and orange marigolds, white, pink, and yellow snapdragons, magenta achilleas, brilliant red zinnias, silvery dusty miller, pink and green alternantheras, cleomes, coleuses, and more.

"It was an even busier garden in Albert's day, chock full of rustic trellises and cedar furniture," former head groundskeeper Chet Davis explains. "We've simplified that a bit. Since then the growing deer population has also become a major problem, so we use repellents and try to eliminate favorite deer foods like petunias, geraniums, pansies, and asters. And of course we fence off new trees and shrubs, though we haven't won the battle yet."

At the far end of the Show Garden is what looks like a great shaggy tree. It turns out to be a rustic, two-story gazebo enveloped in Chinese wisteria vines—a favorite hideaway for guests that is an exact replica of a "prospect tower" from Andrew Jackson Downing's landscaping sketch-book. It is one of more than a hundred gazebos, called "summer houses" at Mohonk, that dot the gardens and trails, offering visitors secluded spots to rest, contemplate views, or read a good book. The charming structures, most made of wood, some of stone, are so ubiquitous that they have become the official emblem of the resort.

Beyond the prospect tower are more floral displays. A Rose Garden memorializing Albert K. Smiley II boasts a variety of hybrid teas. Nearby, old Scotch, sweetbrier, and damask roses grow in a perennial border beside a long arbor covered with wisteria and trumpet creeper, which in turn flanks a large Cutting Garden that supplies flowers for the hotel. On the other side of the arbor the Herb Garden, designed by Ruth Smiley, is full of scented, culinary, and medicinal species, all focused on a millstone made from local rock on which an old bee skep is perched.

From here a path leads over to the Fern/Wildflower Trail, along a small brook through the woods. Thoughtfully labeled for visitors are some 30 different types of ferns, mostly native to the region. Also along the brook are more than a hundred kinds of wild flowers, from Dutchman's breeches, bloodroot, and marsh marigold in spring to gold-enrod, cardinal flower, closed gentian, and celandine later in the year.

Bordering the wild flower trail is one of the many horticultural curiosities in which the Smileys seem to delight: an umbrella magnolia (*Magnolia tripetala*) that normally does not flourish in this climate but at Mohonk has found a friendly, sheltered niche, bearing huge, creamy white flowers among its oversized leaves in June. On your way down to the greenhouses—where thousands of plants are grown for the hotel and gardens, and unusual Victorian-era houseplants are for sale—keep an eye out for other surprises, among them a corkscrew willow with picturesque-ly tortured branches; a dawn redwood, thought extinct until it was found growing in central China a half century ago; and, across the field on the exit road, a colossal, tentlike weeping beech that many visitors, especially kids, consider the most appealing tree on the grounds.

Leave ample time to savor Mohonk's old-fashioned pleasures, and stay for at least a night if you can. The signs on the winding auto road set the tone for any visit. They read: "Slowly and Quietly Please."

MOHONK MOUNTAIN HOUSE,
NEW PALTZ

❖ MOHONK MOUNTAIN HOUSE, Mohonk Lake, New Paltz, NY 12561. Tel. (914) 255-1000 or (800) 772-6646. **Facilities**: Gazebos and benches everywhere provide places to relax. Day visitors can buy lunch and gifts at the Picnic Lodge from June through October, or eat their own picnics nearby. The greenhouse offers cut flowers, dried arrangements,and house plants for sale. The gardens are accessible to the handicapped. **Open**: Daily, year-round. Hotel guests are admitted free at the gate; day visitors pay an admission charge. **Directions**: Take the New York State Thruway to Exit 18, go west on Rte. 299 through New Paltz, proceed for 6 miles and look for the Mohonk sign on the right. By train, take the Hudson line to Poughkeepsie and a taxi from there.

❖

OPUS 40, SAUGERTIES

The ramps and platforms of Harvey Fite's Opus 40 reflect his theatrical background and his love of Mayan ruins. At the center of the earthworks is a 9-ton bluestone column, which stands like an ancient megalith against the Catskill Mountains to the west.

In 1938 Harvey Fite, an energetic actor-turned-sculptor, paid $400 for 12 acres of scrubby woodland in Saugerties, New York, across the Hudson River from Bard College, where he had established and taught a program in fine arts. Using a machete to hack his way into the property, he began building a rustic studio at the lip of an abandoned bluestone quarry, which during the nineteenth century had supplied paving for the sidewalks of New York. To Fite, a member of the Maverick artists' colony in nearby Woodstock, the old pit was a handy source of raw material for his sculpture, which ran to hefty modern figures and groups. He had no idea that one day it would become a gargantuan sculpture in itself.

As he chiseled his figures, Fite began to build a series of pedestals for them out of the quarry's heaps of discarded rubble. He labored alone, meticulously fitting smaller stones into mortarless walls, swinging larger

ones into place with a quarryman's hand winch and wooden boom. The ramps and terraces he created began to reflect his theatrical background, and the elemental power of Mayan ruins that Fite had helped to restore on a working trip to Central America some years before. They also became increasingly sweeping and rhythmical, incorporating steps, passageways, moats, and pools set off by graceful birches and pines.

"He finally realized that the setting was dwarfing his carved pieces, that, in fact, it was becoming the most important sculpture of all," recalls Tad Richards, Fite's stepson. "So he moved them to more suitable settings at the edge of the woods and went on with his work at a huge new scale."

For the centerpiece of his earthworks, which now covered six acres, the sculptor found a nine-ton column of bluestone in a nearby riverbed, hauled it to the site and, using a sturdy A-frame structure and winches, wrestled it upright on the topmost terrace, where it stands like an ancient, brooding megalith against the Catskills to the west. Fite considered carving it but decided to leave well enough alone.

The artist had been laboring on his masterpiece for nearly four decades when, egged on by family and friends to give it a name, he jokingly dubbed it "Opus 40." In the 37th year, 1976, a hard-muscled, 72-year-old Harvey Fite was still putting in a full day's work when the gears on a tractor he was riding suddenly jammed, plunging him over the quarry wall to his death. His extraordinary creation, however, lives on for visitors to marvel at—a Brobdingnagian vision in stone.

❖ OPUS 40 AND THE QUARRYMAN'S MUSEUM, High Woods, Saugerties, NY 12477. Tel. (914) 246-3400. **Facilities**: Gift shop, sculpture gallery, rest rooms, museum of quarrymen's tools. Jazz, folk, and classical concerts are held outdoors on some Saturday afternoons. **Open**: From noon to 5 p.m. on Fridays, Saturdays, and Sundays from Memorial Day weekend through the last weekend in October (some Saturdays may be reserved for concerts or other events—call ahead). Admission charged. **Directions**: New York State Thruway to Exit 20 (Saugerties), west on Rte. 212 for 1.7 miles, left on winding road for 3 miles and look for sign on right

❖

MOUNTAIN TOP
ARBORETUM,
TANNERSVILLE

A personal vision of a very different kind is evident to the north of Opus 40 in Tannersville, where in 1977 Peter and Bonnie Ahrens began clearing the woods near their summer home in the Catskills to grow plants that appealed to them, many of which were thought too tender to survive subzero winters at an elevation of 2,500 feet. The first four years were spent bulldozing forest into meadow, burying stumps, and erecting an electrified, slant-wire fence against hungry deer. Subsequent years have involved finding, installing, and caring for 500 or 600 plantings grouped in different collections—all in terrain where a meager 18 inches of soil is underlain by solid rock.

Today their Mountain Top Arboretum boasts some 300 species and varieties, all neatly labeled with their common and Latin names. Many originated in Japan, Korea, China, and the Soviet Union; others have come from Canada and the Pacific Northwest. Among the collections are eight varieties of flowering crab apples, a dozen varieties of lilacs and eight types of mountain ashes that bear bright berry clusters in shades of pink, orange, yellow, and red. There are also groupings of conifers, beeches, hawthorns, winterberries, dawn redwoods, azaleas, rhododendrons, and other flowering shrubs, and special areas of winter interest devoted to yellow- and red-twigged dogwoods and to trees chosen for their decorative bark.

Near the entrance to the arboretum is a nursery area where the Ahrens grow seedlings in 15 raised beds that can be covered in winter by snow fencing drawn over big wire hoops. Each year they experiment with

*Right: One of the Ahrens'
favorite trees is mountain
ash. They grow eight types,
notable for their bright berry
clusters that come in shades
of red, orange, yellow, and
pink. Below: Near the
arboretum's entrance is a
nursery where the owners
grow different kinds of
seedlings. The beds are
covered in winter by snow
fencing laid over the big
wire hoops.*

something new—exciting varieties of andromeda, mountain laurel, ornamental grasses—keeping meticulous, computerized records of the results.

There are always projects to work on: a lovely pond with water lilies and other aquatic plants; a rock garden that serves as an inviting introduction to a walking trail the owners have cut through the nearby woods.

Let others worry about their retirement years; Bonnie and Peter Ahrens are having fun.

❖ THE MOUNTAIN TOP ARBORETUM, Rte. 23C, Tannersville, NY 12485. Tel. (518) 589-5566. **Facilities:** There are no public facilities at Onteora Arboretum. **Open:** Daily, June through mid-October. Admission free. **Directions:** From the south, take New York State Thruway to Exit 20, go north on Rte. 32, west on Rtes. 32A and 23A to Tannersville, right at traffic light onto Rte. 23C for 2 miles and look for sign on right. From the the north, take Thruway Exit 21 (Catskill), go west on Rte. 23 toward Windham, south on Rte. 32, west on Rte. 23A to Tannersville, right on Rte. 23C for 2 miles and look for sign on right. By bus from Port Authority Bus Terminal, take Adirondak/Trailways (800-858-8555) to Tannersville.

HUDSON WEST

❖

WASHINGTON PARK,
ALBANY

I n the 1860s, inspired in no small measure by New York's Central Park, Albany leaders called for their own "great central park, which will elevate the morale of the whole city and improve our character and reputation abroad." Declared a Professor David Murray before the august Albany Institute: "Men are wiser, better, more temperate, more loving, when they have wandered amid trees and by waterfalls and heard birds sing and children laugh and play."

As a nucleus the city designated Washington Square, an old military parade ground west of downtown, as well as the adjoining State Street burying grounds, from which graves and tombstones would be removed to other sites. To plan their new Washington Park, the city fathers commissioned Central Park's creators, Frederick Law Olmsted and Calvert Vaux, to advise on a general scheme. Detailed design of the park was turned over to Olmsted and Vaux's young protégés John Bogart and John Yapp Culyer, who had helped the firm engineer both Central Park and Brooklyn's Prospect Park before going into business on their own. Much of the credit for realizing the designers' vision goes to William Egerton, Albany's first superintendent of parks, who supervised the work and added improvements over the next four decades.

Though its acreage may be a fraction of the size of its famous predecessor, Washington Park has long been an urban gem and a source of civic joy. Its graveled walks and curving roads, the latter originally laid out as leisurely carriage drives, lead visitors through a gently sculpted landscape of knolls and swales, a pastoral enclave that was carefully isolated from city distractions by dense buffer plantings and dotted with specimen trees of every kind.

A major center of attraction, then as now, is a long 6-acre lake creat-

113

ed by damming Beaver Creek to provide picturesque views, including that of a fine old iron foot bridge that arches from shore to shore. The original Lake House, a lovely Victorian wooden building with a bandstand on top, was the scene of band concerts, swan-boat excursions, and skating parties until it was found to be rotting dangerously; in 1928 it was replaced by a sturdier masonry structure in a festive, if somewhat incongruous, Spanish-Moorish style fashionable at the time. In 1989 a new amphitheater was built into an adjoining hillside to accommodate free open-air concerts and musicals, which draw appreciative crowds during the summer months.

Other innocent Victorian pleasures have disappeared—a croquet lawn, a deer paddock, tropical and aquatic gardens, rustic shelters, a "refectory" where proper Albanians once alighted from their carriages and bicycles for ice cream or lemonade (the croquet ground has been replaced by a brightly colored, if more utilitarian, playground for kids). A grand old focal point, however, still remains: the King Memorial Fountain, centered on a heroic statue of Moses smiting the rock by sculptor J. Massey Rhind, erected in 1893 in honor of a prominent businessman, Rufus King, by one of his sons.

Around the fountain is one of the park's most popular attractions: a circular geometry of formal beds in nineteenth-century "gardenesque" style. Here and elsewhere in the park some 50,000 tulips of 55 varieties are planted each spring to highlight the annual Tulip Festival in early May. When the tulips have faded, they are replaced by 50 kinds of annuals—petunias, marigolds, begonias, cleomes, asters, Mexican poppies, castor beans, hollyhocks—that provide an old-fashioned blaze of color through summer and fall. Elsewhere in the park there is an impressive Civil War Monument (1912) and a figure of Robert Burns (1888).

"A beautiful park in a city is a great moral power," the founders declared in 1863. Though they might not use words quite so solemn, most modern-day Albanians would agree.

❖ WASHINGTON PARK, three blocks west of Empire State Plaza. Administered by Albany Parks and Recreation Department, 7 Hoffman Avenue, Albany, NY 12209. Tel. (518) 434-4181. **Facilities**: Rest

A major focus of Washington Park is its lovely 6-acre lake, fronted by a Lake House that was built in 1928 in Spanish-Moorish style.

rooms in Lake House. **Open**: Daily, sunrise to sunset. Admission free. Albany's annual Tulip Festival, with food, crafts, and free entertainment, is held in the park on Mother's Day weekend in early May. **Directions**: From the south, take the New York State Thruway north to Exit 23, then I-787 to Empire State Plaza Exit. From the west or north, take I-90 east to I-787, then south to Empire State Plaza Exit. By train from Penn Station, take Amtrak to the Albany/Rensslaer station and a taxi from there.

❖

EMPIRE STATE PLAZA, ALBANY

At the close of the Civil War, about the time Albany city fathers were proposing Washington Park, New York State legislators authorized themselves a new home, a grand Capitol building between State Street and Washington Avenue a few blocks to the east. From the laying of the cornerstone in 1871 it would take a total of 5 architects, 28 years, and $25 million to complete—an intricate potpourri of Italian, French, and Romanesque styles hailed as the most expensive, and controversial, building in the United States.

Frederick Law Olmsted had a hand in this project, too, as one of a three-man advisory board called in during construction to help straighten out the mess (another member was the famed architect Henry Hobson Richardson, credited with the Capitol's final design). Olmsted, by now a recognized arbiter of taste in public matters, was also to devise an elaborate landscaping plan. But with the exception of East Capitol Park, a formal approach up State Street finally completed by his firm in 1898, the building remained hemmed in by older structures. Today, however, the old Capitol can be seen in all its ornate glory—in a modern setting of which Olmsted could have scarcely dreamed, but of whose bold scale and civic amenities he might well have approved.

That setting is Empire State Plaza, a $1.7 billion complex of office and cultural buildings designed under the direction of New York City architects Harrison & Abramovitz and erected between 1965 and 1978. Atop three levels of parking and a covered concourse with restaurants, shops, and banks —serving some 12,000 state

office workers and a million or more visitors a year—a 60-acre plaza embraces a series of skyscrapers, esplanades, fountain pools, and gardens that recall the South American capital city of Brasilia and the visions of the architect Le Corbusier.

The scheme was largely the brainchild of the irrepressible Nelson Rockefeller, then serving as governor, who saw in it a way to simultaneously house a burgeoning bureaucracy, rejuvenate an aging downtown, and transform Albany, as he put it, into "the most beautiful capital city in the world." Though early critics derided it as "Rocky's Folly," the plaza, renamed in his honor after his death in 1979, has become a public landscape and tourist magnet of epic dimensions—a "people's plaza" in the fullest sense.

From the old State Capitol, which frames the plaza on the north, a visitor looks down a quarter mile of broad reflecting pools and jetting fountains, which are flanked by marble sitting benches and double rows of Norway maples trimmed into cubes. On the left are the Performing

Norway maples trimmed into boxy shapes line the quarter-mile esplanade of Empire State Plaza. Rising above them is the Performing Arts Center, known as "The Egg." The grand old Capitol building can be glimpsed behind.

EMPIRE STATE PLAZA, ALBANY

Arts Center, better known as "The Egg," and the 42-story Corning Tower, from whose observation deck visitors can look out over the city to the valley and mountains beyond. On the right, four lower, identical office slabs house various state agencies. Terminating the view on the south is the Cultural Education Center, containing New York's State Museum and Library, whose monumental staircase doubles as an outdoor theater for free summer concerts and other events.

The plaza is notable not only for its futuristic sweep but for its collection of contemporary art, which includes such major sculptures as Alexander Calder's *Triangles and Arches*, rising from the reflecting pool in front of the museum, and George Rickey's *Two Lines Oblique*, whose silvery blades swing randomly in the breeze like the beaks of some giant two-headed bird. François Stahly's *Labyrinth*, a large and playful complex of teakwood constructions, forms a three-dimensional sitting garden back of the Corning Tower. Behind the four agency towers are a real playground for children, with its own imaginative equipment, and two intimate, nicely landscaped gardens where their elders can stroll or sit, one of them with a cascading fountain that memorializes policemen from all over the state.

Opposite these, below an open well adjoining the Justice Building, a sunken courtyard with fountain pool, trees, shrubs, and built-in benches pays tribute to New York's casualties in Viet Nam. The old Capitol is flanked by still more gardens from an earlier era: East Capitol Park, where rosebushes frame the approach to the building's entrance steps, and West Capitol Park, a favorite lunch spot for state workers and tourists, with lawns around a central fountain and seasonal floral displays.

❖ EMPIRE STATE PLAZA, Convention and Tourism Administration, Concourse Rm. 110, Empire State Plaza, Albany, NY 12242. Tel. (518) 474-4759 or 2418. **Facilities**: Underground parking below a concourse with shops, restaurants, rest rooms, and a visitor center, which offers self-guiding brochures to the plaza and information on other Albany attractions. Accessible to the handicapped. **Open**: Daily. Admission free. Free hour-long guided tours, outdoor concerts.

Directions: From the south, take the New York State Thruway north to Exit 23, then I-787 to Empire State Plaza Exit. From the west or north, take I-90 east to I-787, then south to Empire State Plaza Exit. By train from Penn Station, take Amtrak to the Albany/Rensslaer station and a taxi from there.

❖

ACADEMY PARK, ALBANY

Often overlooked by the hordes of visitors to Empire State Plaza is a small garden only a block away, in front of Albany's City Hall in Academy Park. Yet to many knowledgeable plant lovers it is the city's horticultural jewel.

In the late 1980s, when members of the Albany Beautification Committee were casting about for ways to mark the city's 300th anniversary, they hit on two ideas. One was a conifer garden, which would not only provide a fine display of shapes, colors, and textures year-round but would show off many varieties suitable for home use. The other was based on an equally popular theme: the preservation and planting of wild species native to New York State.

Thanks to the volunteer leadership of Peter Rumora—an energetic, semiretired businessman and gardening enthusiast—both dreams have come true, and with considerable style. Under Rumora's eye for design and plant selection, and with the help of a donation from the Harriman Trust, the conifer section of the Tricentennial Garden, completed in 1987 and dedicated to the memory of former New York Governor W. Averell Harriman, presents visitors with an array of 225 evergreen cultivars, plus 90 companion plants, including ornamental grasses, heathers, small azaleas and rhododendrons, prickly pear cactus, and flowering bulbs.

In and around the beds are many specimens that make distinctive garden subjects: hemlocks and spruces in dwarf or weeping forms;

Shrubs with yellow, blue, and green foliage adorn the conifer garden. The old Academy Building is seen in the background.

threadleaved arborvitaes, gold-tinted false cypresses, miniature cotoneasters; bristle-cone pines, Swiss stone pines, Japanese umbrella pines. Together with their companions they form a tapestry of foliage color that includes every shade of green as well as blues, grays, reds, yellows, and even white. Most are planted in mounded-up beds—created with loads of rich manure compost, courtesy of the racetrack upriver at Saratoga—which not only display the varieties to good advantage but provide them with deep root space and ample nourishment ("Anyway," says Rumora with a grin, "flat beds can be a bore.")

Next to the conifer garden is the native wild flower garden, completed in 1988 with the support of a local real estate magnate, Irving Kirsh (who marked it with a plaque "To the Fairest Flower of them all, my wife, Elaine.)" Among a hundred New York State species are mayapple, jack-in-the-pulpit, bellwort, and various ferns located in a shady bed. Sunny areas feature evening primroses, daisies, asters, irises, mallows, sunflowers, Turk's-cap lilies, ironweed, orange day lily, black cohosh, rugosa rose, Joe-Pye weed, skull cap, Jerusalem cross, columbine, and more.

From spring through fall the garden is a veritable feast of color, dramatizing the natural gifts of the Hudson region to those who live there, and to those who come from near and far to see the beautiful valley for themselves.

While in the neighborhood, stop behind City Hall to see the memorial garden to Erastus Corning 2nd, longtime mayor of Albany. The garden was designed by the late Mrs. Corning, an expert horticulturist, and has a number of flowering trees, shrubs, a fountain, and teak benches.

❖ ACADEMY PARK, Washington Avenue, Albany, across from City Hall. Administered by the city's parks department and volunteers of the Albany Beautification Committee. **Facilities**: Parking and rest rooms in nearby Empire State Plaza. Accessible to the handicapped. **Open**: Daily. Admission free. **Directions**: See Empire State Plaza, above. Academy Park is a block from the plaza on Washington Ave., facing the East Park entrance to the old State Capitol and the front of City Hall. By train from Penn Station, take Amtrak to the Albany/Rensslaer station and a taxi from there.